Pain That Heals Unforgiveness

Pain That Heals Unforgiveness

How to be Delivered from the Stronghold of Unforgiveness

by
Carliss Cole

© 2023 by Carliss Cole

Scriptures noted are taken from the King James Version of the Holy Bible. Public Domain.

Word definitions taken from the Oxford English Dictionary.

All rights reserved. No part of this book may be reproduced or transmitted in any form, by any means electronic or mechanical, including photocopy, recording, or any information storage or retrieval system, without permission in writing from both the copyright owner and the publisher.

Requests for permission to make copies of any part of this work should be sent to the attention of carlisscoledovewriter@gmail.com.

ISBN: 979-8-218-10938-7

Printed in the United States of America.

Dedication

I want to dedicate this book to all of you who are struggling with unforgiveness in your heart. I am praying for you.

Special Thanks

To my Lord and Savior Jesus Christ. You have always been there for me even when I had unforgiveness in my heart, somehow you still put up with me and loved me through it all. Thank you so much for your love, patience, and kindness towards me, and for being with me through the long haul no matter what I'm going through. My goal is to be like you, where forgiving is no longer a struggle, but becomes a part of who I am. I love you and thank you!

To my love, comforter, and friend, the Holy Spirit. Thank you so much for being ever present in my life, even when I had unforgiveness in my heart. You were still there for me, brushing up against me, waking me up in the morning, yet giving me another chance to forgive those whom I considered unforgiveable. You have been with me through the long haul, and I find comfort in knowing that you will always be with me. For I cannot bear to even breathe without you in my life. I love you and thank you!

To God who is my Heavenly Father. Thank you so much for sending your Son Jesus Christ to die on the cross for my sins and forgive me. You are a constant reminder of the sacrifice of forgiveness. Thank you for being here for me and helping me realize that I must forgive to live. I love you so much and I aim to please you. I aim to glorify you. I aim for your purpose, will, and call on my life to be accomplished in and through me. And my final aim and dream is to see a smile on your face and hear you say well done, so I can live with you forever. You are truly a great Father to me. I love you and thank you!

Thank you to my young lady, my beautiful daughter Angel, who loves and forgives me when I get lost in the ages and stages of her life. Angel you are the best miracle daughter gift God could have ever given me, and I am so grateful that you are my child! I love you and thank you!

Thank you to my young man, my handsome son Andrew, who loves and forgives me when I "Over Motherize" as he calls it. Andrew you are the best miracle son gift God could have ever given me, and I am so grateful that you are my child! I love you and thank you!

Thank you to my late Mother, Gwendolyn Delores Lee, and my late Father, Clarence Bradford Jr. for being the best parents ever! Even though I miss you both so much, your words and teachings have stuck and stayed with me always, reminding me to always walk in love and be free in who God has called, chosen, and created me to be! Your beautiful memories and words will live in my heart forever! I love you both and thank you!

Thank you to my late Pastor, Counselor, Mentor, and Friend, Pastor Omar Morris, of Faith Church. Even though I miss you so much, your words and teachings will always be in my heart. I love you and thank you.

Thank you to my Editor, Kerri Holloway, who worked so hard alongside with me to accomplish this published work. This is the first time I have used an Editor, and I'm so glad that I did. Your professionalism and gift gave me insight and expansion in using my gift, and together our gifts rock and created this beautiful piece of work. You are truly a God send! I enjoyed learning from you and working with you! Thank you so much!

Thank you to my Publisher, Tim Holloway of Witty Writings. I'm so glad to use you to publish my book again. Truly your price and professionalism are amazing! Thank you so much!

Thank you to my illustrator, Mr. Jeffrey Sass. Words cannot explain the remarkable job you did on my book cover. I look forward to working with you in the near future. You Rock!

Thank you to Pastor Elisha Cole for helping me fund my vision in producing this published book. Not only are you a generous giver to the vision of those of us in the Body of Christ, but you are a remarkable father to our children. Thank You So Much!

Thank you to my Pastors, David and Nicole Crank, of Faith Church, and my Faith Church family. I'm so blessed to be a part of the Faith Church family. You were my life support, when I felt like the blows of life was hitting me so hard, that I couldn't breathe. God used your Faith Church to restore me, reignite the passion of God in me, and resurrect the gifts of God in me. This book is the fruit of what God has done in my life, because of the outpouring of love, comfort, support, and healing that I've received from being a part of the Faith Church Family. Thank you so much for all of your love. I love you!

Thank you to my Mentor, who is wise beyond his years. My Brother in Christ, Friend, Motivational Speaker, Pastor, Producer, and Actor, Devon Franklin. You are definitely one of the most inspirational speakers I've heard and learned from. Thank you for all your words of encouragement, as well as your challenging teachings, that has inspired me to push forward and accomplish my goals, with integrity, in some of the most difficult times in my life. Thank you for sharing your Beautiful Mother and Aunts with ME! "It Takes A Woman." Their Godly Wisdom has given me courage to be a better ME! Thanks Devon, and as you always say to everyone "I love you and there's nothing you can do about it!"

Thank you to all of you who have been so encouraging and supportive in my life, from pastors, teachers, family and friends to former coworkers and those who even supported me on social media. I am truly blessed! Thank you and I love you!

May this book be a blessing to all of you, as much as you have been a blessing to me!

Thank you and I love you all!

Table of Contents

Introduction	. . . .	1
Chapter 1	Pain That Heals Unforgiveness in Your Childhood	3
Chapter 2	Pain That Heals Unforgiveness in Your Teenage Years	21
Chapter 3	Pain That Heals Unforgiveness in Your Relationships	37
Chapter 4	Pain That Heals Unforgiveness in Your Heart	51
Chapter 5	It's Time to Forgive Yourself	63
Chapter 6	It's Time to Forgive God: Getting to the Root of Unforgiveness	79

Chapter 7	You Are Forgiven! Dealing With the Scribes and Pharisees / Your Haters	105
Chapter 8	You Are Healed! You Are an Overcomer	117
Chapter 9	A New Beginning: the Benefits of Forgiveness and Freedom	127
Conclusion	....	141
References	....	145
Quoted Scriptures	....	147

Introduction

My first book, *Pain That Heals*, was published in 2011. I thought it was my last, but in 2020, God told me to write this book, *Pain That Heals Unforgiveness*. Of course God did a complete cleansing in my life of every area within me where unforgiveness was hidden, lying quietly dormant, causing me to believe that I had forgiven. But, when tests came, I realized that I hadn't forgiven in those areas of my life at all. This complete cleansing from all the areas of unforgiveness in my life literally took years.

So I decided to surrender to God. I allowed him to change my agenda, and I submitted to this process of healing from unforgiveness in my life. Sometimes I forgave painfully, meaning I felt the ache of letting go of the unforgiveness that I shouldn't have held on to for so long in the first place.

And then sometimes I didn't even feel the sting of deciding to forgive, which made me wonder why I didn't forgive in that area in the first place. However, I forgave; with no regret and no strings attached, the way God wanted me to.

Afterwards, much to my surprise, this book, *Pain That Heals Unforgiveness*, was birthed through me, and out of me, because God had you in mind.

He knows what you have been through, and he knows what you are going through right now that causes you to struggle with forgiveness. Don't be hard on yourself and condemn yourself. That's not what this book is about.

In this book, God is going to hold your hand, and lovingly guide you through your life, from your childhood on up to now, and help you come face to face with the painful areas in your life that's causing you to have a difficult time forgiving. Then God is going to lovingly show you how to forgive in those areas, so that you can be healed. I encourage you to keep a pen or pencil close by just in case you want to journal your thoughts at the end of each Chapter. I would even suggest having a box of tissue near you, because your healing will be emotional as well. Nevertheless you will be healed.

For your enjoyment in reading this book, along with the teachings about healing from unforgiveness, the Lord has also impressed upon my heart to use a few scenarios as examples concerning different issues and actions that occur in everyday life and relationships.

All the scenarios and names used are imaginary, which means they are not real. Hopefully, the teachings, imaginary characters, and situations written in this book will help you get a better understanding of what's going on in your own personal life and how you can manage those issues and difficult situations, with an open heart to forgive, which is according to the Word of God (the Bible). Only when you're able to forgive will you experience the *Pain That Heals Unforgiveness*.

When this happens in your life, that's when God will be glorified in you and through you so that you can help many others also experience the *Pain That Heals Unforgiveness*. It's time to read and be healed!

Carliss Cole

CHAPTER 1

Pain That Heals Unforgiveness in Your Childhood

Scenario 1: Skylar and her dad's mistress

Skylar is having a tantrum. She and her dad are at a woman's house, whom her dad calls his "friend." She just feels something is not right about her dad visiting this "friend" of his. Skylar is having strange feelings that she doesn't understand, even though she is just 5 years old. Skylar's dad is married to her mother, and she has a lot of fun when she spends time with both her mom and dad together, but she doesn't feel the same way when she's spending time with her dad and this "friend" of his. In fact, she feels so uncomfortable, that she moves a lot, whines, complains, and irritates her dad to the point that he makes her take a nap at his "friend's" house.

His "friend" is nice to her, but Skylar doesn't want to be nice to the woman.

Skylar, her dad, and his "friend" are watching a movie, and Skylar starts moving again, then she gets up and turns to look at her dad.

    Skylar: "Daddy I want to go home!"

> **Dad:** "Just wait a minute Sky, let's wait until this movie goes off."

Skylar starts whining.

> **Skylar:** "Daddy, I don't want to wait to this movie goes off…I want to go home and be with Momma right now…"

Dad picks Skylar up and sits his daughter on his lap.

> **Dad:** "I promise you Sky, if you'll be good, I will take you to our favorite food place when this movie goes off!"

Skylar hugs her dad and jumps off of his lap and cheers.

> **Skylar:** "Yaaaay! Daddy!"

Dad hugs and kisses her, then Skylar sits back down on the couch next to her Dad to watch the movie.

Dad's phone rings, and he looks at the number, then goes into the other room.

Skylar and Dad's "friend" hear him arguing on the phone with Skylar's Mom. Skylar looks over at her dad's "friend" and begins to talk to her.

> **Skylar:** "My mom and dad are always fussing at each other, and I don't know why. Do you know why?"

> **Dad's "friend":** "No."

> **Skylar:** "I don't know either. It makes me so sad. I wish they got along."

Skylar's dad comes back in the living room and sits down. He puts Skylar back on his lap and continues to watch the movie.

Skylar's eyes get heavy, so she puts her head on Dad's shoulder and falls asleep.

Hours pass and Skylar wakes up in the morning, rubbing her eyes. She doesn't even realize that she spent the night at her dad's "friend" house again. Skylar hears laughing in the other room, so she tiptoes toward the room, slowly opens the door, and peeks in. She sees her dad and his "friend" kissing. She notices that her dad is kissing his "friend" like he kisses her mom, his wife. Instantly Skylar reacts.

Skylar: "NOOOOOOO!!!!!"

Skylar takes off running, her dad immediately realizes that Skylar saw what he did, so he quickly jumps up and begins to chase her around the house.

Dad: "Sky! Stop running! Stop screaming!"

Skylar continues to run, and she screams louder.

Skylar: "NO DADDY! YOU KISSED YOUR FRIEND LIKE YOU KISS MOM! NOOOOOO! NOOOOOO!"

He finally catches her, but Skylar is trying to break away from him, kicking and screaming.

Skylar: "NO! YOU KISSED YOUR FRIEND! I WILL NEVER FORGIVE YOU DAD!"

Skylar went home and told her mother what happened, and her parents argued even more for the next few years, because her dad continued to see his "friend." No matter how much Skylar prayed that Dad would stop cheating on Mom so her parents could finally be together and happy, he never stopped cheating, so eventually her mom filed for divorce.

Skylar's dad was so angry that he tried to gain full custody of Skylar, but failed because she insisted on staying with her mom full-time. She only saw her dad on weekends, and only if his "friend" wasn't with them.

This agreement worked for a while, but eventually it stopped because he gradually stopped picking her up on weekends, to the point that she didn't see or hear from her dad anymore.

For years Skylar never forgot when she saw her dad kiss another woman, the same way he kissed her mom while they were still married. Sometimes Skylar wondered if it was her fault that her parents divorced. Maybe if she hadn't told her mom what happened that day, her parents would still be together.

* * *

I'm going to pause right here just to let you know, the bad things that happened to you as a child: that molestation and rape, when you were bullied in school, your parent's divorce, those parents who walked out and left you to be raised in foster home(s) or be adopted, is not your fault. *It is not your fault. God wants to set you free right now from your childhood trauma. He is letting you know today that it is not your fault.*

People hurt you when you were a child because those people were hurt by someone else, and they never confronted their pain, so they took their pain out on you. *But you must know that it is not your fault.*

Why am I choosing to say that *it IS not your fault, instead of, it WAS not your fault?* Sure, I can answer that for you. I'm saying *IS,* instead of *WAS,* because many of you see the pain that you have gone through as if it *IS,* still happening, not *WAS* happening, and God wants to let you know that what you went through as a child, *it IS over*! God wants to heal you from your childhood trauma.

Going through all of this since her childhood really traumatized Skylar and left her in a state of unforgiveness and rebellion towards her dad. As Skylar grew older, the memory of seeing him kiss another woman while still married to her mom, her parent's divorce, and the custody battle, replayed in her mind over and over.

As a result, Skylar started doing whatever she wanted to do, and did not care who she hurt in the process. She had a lot of anger, hurt and pain of unforgiveness in her heart towards her dad. She felt so rejected by him. How could he just give up on her, and stop seeing her?

In spite of Skylar's unforgiveness towards her dad, and her careless lifestyle, God showed his love towards her. She was hired for a great job, were she met a friend who invited her to church. Skylar's life was forever changed. She received Jesus into her heart and life, and she began to go to church on a regular basis.

Skylar's life moved forward in every area, except in relationships with men. Her problem was, like her dad, she didn't keep her commitments, so she cheated on men.

As she began to see this pattern persist in her life, she decided to go to counseling and therapy, while continuing to go to work and church. She discovered her pattern of lack of commitment in relationships had to do with unforgiveness towards her dad for cheating on her mom, and she was still hurting from the memory of him leaving her.

Skylar took a few minutes every day to spend time with God, and with the help of her counselors and therapists, she reached out to her dad's sister, to reconnect with him. When she found him, she asked if he would go to counseling with her. When he did, Skylar confronted her pain and told him how hurt she was, only to find out that he had caught his own mother—Skylar's grandmother—cheating on his father when he was a child. Her dad was still trapped in that painful memory, even though his parents had already passed.

Skylar and her dad received healing at the same time, giving her a strong relationship with both of her parents. His "friend" left him to be with another man. Her mom forgave her dad. Her parents started going to counseling together, then began dating, and eventually decided to get remarried.

Skylar was so happy that her childhood prayers finally came to pass. Her parents were back together. Skylar's pattern of not being committed in relationships ended; she was completely healed. However, she decided to live the single life for a while so she could spend more time with her dad. They hung out more than they ever had before. God healed and restored Skylar's relationship with him.

I know there is something you experienced as a child that hurt you deeply. Many of you who are reading this book were traumatized as a child.

Some of you all were exposed to things in life at an early age that you should not have been exposed to, like Skylar was. I know you would rather not confront your childhood trauma head-on, but it is imperative that you do.

> "Facing your pain head-on simply means you are willing to admit it exists in your life. Even though that is a simple task, it is one of the hardest things for us as human beings to do."
>
> (Carliss Cole, *Pain That Heals*, 2011, p.60)

I want to encourage you, instead of running from your pain, to confront your pain head-on. Otherwise, like Skylar, you will have triggers of that pain, causing you to respond as if what you experienced during childhood is still taking place in your present relationships.

When pain is not confronted, it will cause you to not trust anyone, yet you will hold onto that old pain from your past because it's so familiar to you.

> "We tend to put our trust in this pain rather than in the Lord of hosts, who is the healer of all pain."
>
> (Carliss Cole, *Pain That Heals*, 2011, p.17)

Also, not confronting this pain will have you run right into the arms of negative relationships and situations that you were trying to avoid in the first place, which brings even more pain for you.

> "This pain has a tendency to lead and guide us in our everyday lives, without us consciously knowing it. It affects who we choose as friends and with whom we form close relationships. In other words, this pain, without even realizing it, effectively "directs our paths", instead of the Lord directing our paths."
>
> (Carliss Cole, *Pain That Heals*, 2011, p.16)

But thank God that when you picked up this book, you decided you want to be healed and experience the *Pain That Heals Unforgiveness*. Because of that, your healing will manifest before your own eyes, and you will be able to help someone else who is battling with the same struggles as you.

Loved one, I know you believe that the pain you experienced in your childhood will never go away, but according to God's Word you are healed! You're just going through the process right now.

But he was wounded for our transgressions, he was bruised for our iniquities; the chastisement of our peace was upon him; and with his stripes we are healed.

Isaiah 53:5

I know many of you may be wondering why did you go through all of that trauma as a child? **John 10:10** tells you why.

The thief cometh not, but for to steal, and to kill, and to destroy:

John 10:10a

Yes, even in your childhood, the thief—who is our enemy the devil—comes only to steal, kill, and destroy: your peace, your self-esteem, and anything good and godly that's in you and connected to you. But he never wins because Jesus has the final say.

I am come that they might have life, and that they might have it more abundantly.

John 10:10b

This is God's goal and plan for your life! Now let's look at the word **ABUNDANTLY!**

ABUNDANTLY means: fully, fulfilling, meaningfully, fruitfully, plentifully, extremely, exceptionally,

tremendously, immensely, hugely, remarkably, outstandingly, and exceedingly.

Yes! Jesus died on the cross so you can have a healed and ABUNDANT LIFE!

This is also found in **Ephesians 3:20** for my readers that need to be more convinced that Jesus wants you to live **ABUNDANTLY.**

Now unto him that is able to do exceeding abundantly above all that we ask or think, according to the power that worketh in us.
Ephesians 3:20

Beloved, I wish above all things that thou mayest prosper and be in health, even as thy soul prospereth *[keeps prospering forever]*.
3 John 2

Loved one, this book is another reminder to you that God loves you and he wants you to be *healed, whole, and live a prosperous abundant life!*

Loved one, you may look at your life, and see the opposite of what the Word of God says you are. Don't go by what you see. Go by what the Word says, because what the Word says will manifest before your eyes and come to pass!

For we walk by faith, not by sight.
2 Corinthians 5:7

So even though your life may look like it's not going like what you have planned because of what you went through and what you are going through, according to God's plan for your life *You are going to have an ABUNDANT LIFE and prosper! A life you can look forward to everyday!*

For I know the thoughts that I think toward you, saith the LORD, thoughts of peace, and not of evil, to give you an expected *[a life to look forward to everyday]* end *[result]*.
Jeremiah 29:11

SELF-REFLECTION

Do not trivialize how you feel, no matter how others may feel about it. If it's important to you, it's important to God**

Self-Reflection is for the purpose of helping you acknowledge your past and start the healing process in your life. Trauma is something bad that happened to you—or around you—and affected you negatively.

It's important that you recognize your trauma triggers and confront them, because when you ignore them, the healing process cannot take place. When the healing process does not take place, the following problems will occur:

- Surprise behaviors/reactions that seem unrelated to the current situation (explained in detail in my first book, *Pain That Heals*)
- Major overreactions/problems with authority
- Unable to trust anyone
- Seem to always befriend people who take advantage of you

** Please do not be ashamed, embarrassed, or feel guilty for answering any of the Self-Reflection questions honestly. It is very important to be honest so you can be healed. Journaling will aid in your healing and is for your own confidentiality, which cannot be shared unless you choose to share it. A special prayer, resources about who can help, and encouraging scriptures are provided after you complete the Self-Reflection portion of this chapter.

SELF-REFLECTION – JOURNAL

What childhood trauma came to your mind after reading this chapter?

Did this childhood trauma cause patterns in your life? If so, what were the patterns in your childhood?

Do you still see those patterns in your life today? Explain.

How do you think your childhood trauma has affected you (relationships, situations, decision making, etc.)?

Do you find it hard to trust people? Explain.

Has this chapter helped you to understand yourself and your childhood trauma more? If so, how?

Are you ready to forgive the people who caused your childhood trauma? Why or Why not?

If you are still struggling with unforgiveness concerning your childhood trauma, here's a special prayer for you:

*Dear Heavenly Father,
I make the decision today to forgive everyone who has hurt me when I was a child. Lord, I accept the truth that many of them were hurt themselves and that's why they hurt me. Therefore, Lord, I forgive them, and I will no longer walk in the pain of unforgiveness from my childhood, but I receive the* Pain That Heals Unforgiveness *from my childhood, by using my painful experiences to help others who are experiencing pain from their childhood right now. Thank you, Lord, for healing me.
In Jesus' Name! Amen.*

While you are praying to be healed from your pain, it is also important to work on yourself as well, by getting and receiving the help you need **(James 2:17)**.

You were not meant to walk through life alone. If you are still experiencing any triggers, realizing painful patterns and behaviors, and are struggling from your childhood trauma, please pray to God. If you are having a hard time praying to God, you can start by praying The Lord's Prayer **(Matthew 6:9-13).** God will lead you from there.

Then talk to someone, like a friend or relative that you can trust. You can also contact your Pastor (Pastor's Team), a Youth Pastor, a Counselor, a Therapist, or Group Therapist. These resources can be found through some employers, and also in your community, at schools and churches, sometimes for a minimum fee or even free! They will help keep you personally accountable as well. Be encouraged! God is going to work all things together for your good **(Romans 8:28).**

Know that once you decide to forgive, the process of forgiveness begins. No matter how long it takes, God will complete his work of forgiveness in you **(Philippians 1:6).**

Psalm 34:17 – The righteous cry, and the Lord heareth, and delivereth them out of all their troubles.

Matthew 21:22 – And all things, whatsoever ye shall ask in prayer, believing, ye shall receive.

James 5:16 – Confess your faults one to another, and pray one for another, that ye may be healed. The effectual fervent prayer of a righteous man availeth much.

Proverbs 11:14 – Where no counsel is, the people fall: but in the multitude of counsellors there is safety.

Romans 8:28 – And we know that all things work together for good to them that love God, to them who are the called according to his purpose.

James 2:17 – Even so faith, if it hath not works, is dead, being alone.

Philippians 1:6 – Being confident of this very thing, that he which hath begun a good work in you will perform it until the day of Jesus Christ.

CHAPTER 2

Pain That Heals Unforgiveness in your Teenage Years

Scenario 2: Scott fights bullies at his new school

Scott is the new guy at his high school. His family moved from St. Louis, Missouri, to San Francisco, California, because his dad received a job promotion. Even though Scott really likes San Francisco, he doesn't want to stay there because all of his family and friends are in St. Louis.

What Scott *really* doesn't like is being the new guy at his high school. He didn't grow up with any of the kids there. The California girls are pretty, smart and they seem to like him a lot, but Scott feels like the guys are mean bullies who hate to see him coming. Scott doesn't know how he's going to make friends at his new high school.

The first month of attending school was the hardest. Scott dealt with being bullied every day. He told his parents, but his dad couldn't take off of work, because his new job promotion didn't allow him to take days off for the first year. Scott's mom had gotten a new job too, so she couldn't take off of work either. Both of Scott's parents believed that the bullying would eventually stop; they felt that bullying wasn't uncommon for new kids.

Scott stopped trying to get his parents to listen to him. So instead, one day he decided that he was going to fight back. After all, a month of bullying was too much, and it had already built up a lot of anger in him.

Monday came back around, and Scott was ready to fight. While he was walking down the hall with two girls, one on each side of him, one of the bullies bumped into him and made him drop all of his books. This wasn't the first time that happened to him, but this time Scott responded.

> **Scott:** "MAN, YOU HAVE A PROBLEM?!"
>
> **Bully 1:** "DO YOU?"
>
> **Scott:** "YEA, I HAVE A PROBLEM WITH YOU BUMPING INTO ME!"
>
> **Bully 2:** "YOU BUMPED INTO HIM!"
>
> **Scott:** "MAN, NO I DIDN'T! FORGET IT!"

Scott hit Bully 1 in his jaw, and he fell to the floor. Bully 2 tried to come for him, and Scott punched him, knocking the second bully down to the floor. By then the Principal came to stop the fight.

> **Principal:** "YOU THREE! COME TO MY OFFICE! NOW!"

Later that evening Scott and his parents are all at the dinner table silently eating. Normally there's a lot of conversation going on, but the Principal already called his parents about the fight and suspension from school. Scott decides to break the silence.

Scott: "Mom…Dad…I'm sorry I got suspended today."

Dad: "Well son you should be! I didn't move us up here to California for you to start getting into fights at school!"

Mom: "Scotty what happened? You could've talked to us about it."

Scott: "I tried, but you were too busy working and both of you didn't take me seriously enough to take off from work. You didn't listen…"

Mom: "I'm sorry son, I thought that it would just go away. Some kids normally bully new kids, but eventually they stop. I remember getting bullied by girls at my new middle school, but later we became the best of friends Scotty."

Scott: "Well Mom, things are a lot different since the time you were in school!"

Dad: "Scott you should know how to conduct yourself! We taught you how to conduct yourself!"

Scott: "I should know how to conduct myself around kids I don't know at all? Kids who are bullying me? Dad, do you know how it feels to be bullied?"

Dad look away from his son, with a serious but sad look.

> **Scott:** "Yea, I didn't think so, the way you just moved me and Mom out here! Mom had to find a new job, and you want me to pretend like I'm okay with just leaving my family and friends in St. Louis, without you asking me or Mom how we feel about it! But I'M THE ONE who doesn't know how to act? I just lost my appetite! Sorry Mom, I'm not hungry anymore!"

Scott leaves and goes to his room and slams the door behind him.

> **Mom:** "Scotty!"
>
> **Dad:** "Son you better get back down here and eat your dinner!!"

The table is silent again. Scott's mom is looking at his dad sadly.

> **Mom:** "Why didn't you tell Scotty? It's as if you forgot. Talk to your son honey."
>
> **Dad:** "I don't want to talk about it. Those four years in high school, were and still are, the worst years of my life."
>
> **Mom:** "I know. I was there then, and I'm here now. Your son needs to hear that his parents know how he feels being bullied at school."
>
> **Dad:** "I just want my son to be tougher than me! I was a wimp! I allowed those bullies to get to me so

bad that I start drinking alcohol and taking drugs. I hate I let those bullies get to me that bad. I spent years of my life taking you through so much and going through recovery programs. That's why I work so hard to make sure you and Scott have the best."

Mom: "I know you do honey. And I don't regret one moment with you. Look at you now. God has brought you a long way, so you have nothing to be ashamed of. What you went through does not define who you are."

Dad: "Thank you Sweetie, I'm so glad you stood by my side through it all."

They hug and kiss.

Mom: "I have the best husband in the world indeed; he is handsome, smart, wise, and has the courage to tell his son everything he has just told me. When you do that, you will stop our son from making the same mistakes you made when you were bullied. You know how being bullied can cause a person to make harmful choices. You know that when you go to get help by talking to people you trust, it will save your life too. God didn't just use me to help save your life, God used Pastors, Counselors, Therapists, and the list goes on and on. So just in case our Scotty feels he can't talk to us, we need to let him know that we are ok with him talking to someone who will help him, because we don't want him to try to deal with it on his own. So are you ready honey?"

Dad: "Thanks Sweetie, I needed that. You should have been a Counselor…Yes, I'm ready."

Mom: "Ok, I'll go get him from his room."

* * *

Scott is really hurt because he feels like he wasn't heard. He feels that if his parents would have listened to him, he would have not been in that bad situation at school.

Have you ever felt that way as a teenager? Or, if you are a teenager now, do you ever feel that way? Have you ever felt like you were being overlooked, ignored, not seen, or heard? Did you start making decisions that could have caused you harm, and others too?

That's why it's important you know that Jesus hears you. Sometimes the people closest to you may not hear you the way you want to be heard. They may not see you the way you want to be seen. They may not even understand you the way you would like to be understood. But God does. He hears, sees, and understands you just the way you need him to, each and every time you pray and call upon him.

For the eyes of the Lord are over the righteous, and his ears are open unto their prayers...

1 Peter 3:12a

And if we know that he hear us, whatsoever we ask, we know that we have the petitions that we desired of him.

1 John 5:15

Then shall ye call upon me, and ye shall go and pray unto me, and I will hearken unto you. And ye shall seek me, and find me, when ye shall search for me with all your heart.

Jeremiah 29:12-13

As a teenager, Scott had no idea that he could call on God when he was being bullied at school. And many of us didn't know that we could call on God when we were going through our teenage years. Even though some of us went to church, we didn't have a personal relationship with God.

Going to church and learning about Jesus is good, and can be fun too! Even though it's important to continue to go to church, it's just as important to have your own personal relationship with Jesus Christ.

It's only in that personal relationship with Jesus Christ that you will feel comfortable enough to talk to Jesus about anything and everything as a child, teenager, and an adult.

Then, and only then, will you have confidence in knowing he will answer when you call out to him.

Talking to God and having a personal relationship with Jesus Christ is so important, because he will lead and guide you about whom you should talk to. Sometimes God will put on your heart someone you already trust, and sometimes he will just bring their name up in a conversation you may be having with a family member or friend, who highly recommends them. You may meet someone at church, school, or work that either you are comfortable talking to, or who will help you find a good Counselor, Therapist, or Pastor to talk to. You will definitely know who you can trust if you ask God and spend time with him.

Having a relationship with God, and talking to someone (people) whom God leads and whom you trust is also important because it will remove any type of shame and guilt that tries to plague your life. It doesn't matter what happened in your past. Whatever you did, or may be doing right now, because of some painful experience as a teenager—or even if you're experiencing something painful as an adult now—just know that God doesn't want you to feel guilty about the decisions you've made that were wrong.

Of course there's no way you can go back and change those wrong decisions you made or the people who have hurt you as a teenager, so don't even try. Just know that God doesn't want you to carry the pain of unforgiveness in your heart towards yourself or anyone else who hurt you in your teenage years.

God wants to heal you. What you experienced in your teenage years, or may be going through now as a teenager, does not define who you are, and the amazing destiny God has planned for your life. Please do not live in condemnation. Receive Jesus in your heart and the love he gives to you. Then walk in the freedom that salvation brings to you.

For God sent not his Son into the world to condemn the world; but that the world through him might be saved.
John 3:17

Scott felt so much better after his parents talked to him. He was really amazed to hear how his father overcame bullying and everything else he went through as a result of being bullied. Both of Scott's parents went to his school to address the bullying problem that many students were having. Scott gained more confidence and realized if his parents overcame bullying, he could too. He felt safer at school and start talking to students in his classes more, because he knew that if anyone bullied him again, his parents would come and address it quickly.

Scott's parents decided to create a special committee to end bullying at his high school.

Then, Scott and his parents decided to go further by receiving Family Counseling and Therapy. They decided to not only seek God for themselves, but pray together as well, while they continued going to church as a family.

Scott's family grew closer to each other, the church, school, and their new community.

SELF-REFLECTION

Do not trivialize how you feel, no matter how others may feel about it. If it's important to you, it's important to God**

Self-reflection is for the purpose of helping you acknowledge your past and start the healing process in your life. Trauma is something bad that happened to you—or around you—and affected you negatively.

It's important that you recognize your trauma triggers and confront them, because when you ignore them, the healing process cannot take place. When the healing process does not take place, the following problems will occur:

- Surprise behaviors/reactions that seem unrelated to the current situation (explained in detail in my first book, *Pain That Heals*)
- Major overreactions/problems with authority
- Unable to trust anyone
- Seem to always befriend people who take advantage of you

** Please do not be ashamed, embarrassed, or feel guilty for answering any of the Self-Reflection questions honestly. It is very important to be honest so you can be healed. Journaling will aid in your healing and is for your own confidentiality, which cannot be shared unless you choose to share it. A special prayer, resources about who can help, and encouraging scriptures are provided after you complete the Self-Reflection portion of this chapter.

SELF-REFLECTION – JOURNAL

What teenage trauma comes to mind after reading this chapter?

Did this teenage trauma cause patterns in your life? If so, what were the patterns during your teenage years?

Do you still see those patterns in your life today? Explain.

How do you think your teenage trauma has affected you (relationships, situations, decision making, etc.)?

Has your teenage trauma caused you to have a hard time trusting people? Explain.

Has reading this chapter helped you to understand yourself and your teenage trauma more? If so, how?

Are you ready to forgive the people who caused trauma during your teenage years? Why or Why not?

Are you ready to forgive yourself for the wrong decisions you made in your teenage years that caused trauma in your life? Why or Why not? *(this question does not apply to those who were victimized during their teenage years)*

If you are still struggling with unforgiveness from Teenage Trauma, here's a special prayer for you.

*Dear Heavenly Father,
I make the decision today to forgive everyone who has hurt me when I was a teenager (or those who are hurting and bullying me now as a teenager).
Lord, I accept the truth that many of them were hurt themselves, and that's why they hurt me.
Therefore, Lord, I forgive them, and I will no longer walk in the pain of unforgiveness in my teenage years,*

but I receive the Pain That Heals Unforgiveness
*by using my painful experiences to help others who are
in pain from their teenage years right now.
Thank you, Lord, for healing me!
In Jesus' Name! Amen!*

While you are praying to be healed from your pain, it is important to work on yourself, by getting and receiving the help you need **(James 2:17).**

You were not meant to walk through life alone. If you are struggling with being bullied during your teenage years, or, if you are still experiencing any of these triggers, such as: social isolation, feelings of shame, sleep disturbance, changes in eating habits, low self-esteem, anxiety, skipping school, poor performance in school, or other related signs, please pray to God, and seek help. If you are having a hard time praying to God, you can start by praying The Lord's Prayer **(Matthew 6:9-13).** God will lead you from there.

Then talk to someone, like a friend or relative that you can trust. You can also contact your Pastor (Pastor's Team), a Counselor, a Therapist, or Group Therapist. These resources can be found through some employers, and also in your community, at schools and churches, and sometimes for a minimum fee or even free! Be encouraged! God will work all things together for your good **(Romans 8:28).**

Know that once you decide to forgive, the process of forgiveness begins. No matter how long it takes, God will complete his work of forgiveness in you **(Philippians 1:6).**

Psalm 34:17 – The righteous cry, and the LORD heareth, and delivereth them out of all their troubles.

Matthew 21:22 – And all things, whatsoever ye shall ask in prayer, believing, ye shall receive.

James 5:16 – Confess your faults one to another, and pray one for another, that ye may be healed. The effectual fervent prayer of a righteous man availeth much.

Proverbs 11:14 – Where no counsel is, the people fall: but in the multitude of counsellors there is safety.

Romans 8:28 – And we know that all things work together for good to them that love God, to them who are the called according to his purpose.

James 2:17 – Even so faith, if it hath not works, is dead, being alone.

Philippians 1:6 – Being confident of this very thing, that he which hath begun a good work in you will perform it until the day of Jesus Christ.

36

CHAPTER 3

Pain That Heals Unforgiveness in Relationships

Scenario 3: Casey and Sarah, workplace BFF's

Casey and Sarah have been best buddies at work for over five years. They have worked on the same Advertising Team the entire time, with Casey as the Team Leader. Even though they really enjoy their work friendship, their personal lives give them no leisure time to hang out with each other outside of the office. So when they get off of work, they don't see each other until they go back to work the next day, and they're both fine with that.

One day Sarah brings a project in that she has been working on all night at home. She is excited and she knows that Casey is going to be excited when she sees it too.

Sarah: "Hey lady! How are you doing today?"

Casey: "Okay…I guess…"

Sarah: "Well, I have something to show you that will make you feel much better. Here ya go!"

Sarah shows Casey her new Marketing Ad Project poster, with a big smile on her face. Casey looks at it and says nothing. Sarah's smile slowly goes into a frown.

Sarah: "What's up with you today?"

Casey: "Nothing…it's just not…marketable to me, that's all."

Sarah: "What?! I was up all night doing this! And Casey we have the same eye for good marketing…so what's wrong?"

Casey: "Oh…something's gotta be wrong with me because I don't like your ad?"

Sarah: "Uuuhhh yeah!"

Casey: (waves Sarah off) "Whatever Sarah…and what I don't understand is that you didn't even ask me if I wanted to help!"

Sarah: "Uuuhhh no! I didn't ask you to help me this time. Whenever I ask, you're ALWAYS busy when we get off of work."

Casey: "You still could have asked me…"

Sarah: "You still haven't told me, what's up with your attitude this morning?"

Casey: "I just don't like it…that's all I'm saying. Can I have my own opinion for once?"

Sarah: "Well, if you don't like it, I'm going to show Mr. Gregory."

Casey: "Oh, so even though I'm YOUR LEAD on our marketing team…you're still gonna go to our boss?"

Sarah: "Yelp! Casey, I don't know what's going on with you this morning, but I'm not gonna allow you to mess up what could be really good money for me, even for YOU, and our marketing team, as well as for this company."

Casey: "If you go to Mr. Gregory, I will put you off of my team!"

Sarah: "BYE!"

Sarah leaves Casey's office.

Now, let's go back and find out what really happened to Casey earlier that morning before *Sarah came to work.*

The boss, Mr. Gregory, has his secretary call Casey into his office for a brief unscheduled meeting. Casey is so excited because she has been expecting a raise for quite some time now. Casey believes that this is finally the moment she's been waiting for!

Mr. Gregory: "I'm sorry that this meeting is unscheduled."

Casey: "No! No! No apology needed! I've been waiting for this meeting for quite some time now."

Mr. Gregory: (shrugs uncomfortably in his chair, and clears his throat) "There have been some changes in the company, due to the pandemic that has affected all of us. I'm so glad that I didn't have to lay off one of my best workers…"

Casey: (interrupts) "And I truly thank you for that Mr. Gregory!"

Mr. Gregory: (clearing his throat again) "You're quite welcome…"

Silence. Then Mr. Gregory continues.

Mr. Gregory: "However, I will not be able to give you a salary raise, even though you deserve it. And I'm going to have to demote you from being one of my Team Leaders, to just being on the team, like the other workers. This company can no longer pay the salary of Marketing Team Leaders."

Casey: (stops smiling, now with tears in her eyes) "Mr. Gregory I thought you said in our last meeting…"

Mr. Gregory: (interrupts) "I know what I said Casey, and I apologize that I have to do this. But I have to do what's best for this company, and that doesn't just include you. That includes your co-workers also."

Casey: (shocked, sad, silently angry, hurt) "Wow! Just when I thought I was going to finally earn enough money to take care of my sick mother, and even have some extra change for my children…"

Mr. Gregory finally breaks the uncomfortable silence.

Mr. Gregory: (clearing his throat) "I'm…I'm sorry…but I have to get back to work now."

Casey slowly gets up and leaves Mr. Gregory's office, walks back to her own office and sits at her desk. Sarah walks in excitedly, with her new Marketing Ad Project …

* * *

Many times the pain we experience in our relationships has a lot to do with hidden pain, either from our past or that is happening in our lives now. This is why it is so important to get to the root of our pain.

> "The root of your pain is always in connection with certain relationships or circumstances."
>
> (Carliss Cole, *Pain That Heals*, 2011, p.30)

The real reason for Casey's attitude toward Sarah was her hurt about the decision their boss made to demote her position and salary, after he'd promised her a raise. When their boss broke his promise to Casey, that triggered her questioning Sarah's loyalty toward her as a friend.

However, Sarah can tell something is wrong with her friend, noticing that Casey wasn't expressing herself like she normally would. Sarah cared enough to turn back around before going into Mr. Gregory's office, and instead, she goes back into Casey's office and asks more questions.

* * *

Sarah: "Casey, what's wrong? Please talk to me."

Casey: "I don't want to talk. I thought you were going to Mr. Gregory's office to show off your…your…. new…whatever..."

Sarah: "I changed my mind. You mean more to me than a new Marketing Ad Project. When we win, we win together Casey. It's not winning without you."

Silence. Casey begins to cry.

Casey : "It hurts to think about it…it hurts to talk about it…"

Sarah: "I know, but Casey you have to. I'm your friend. I may be your best friend at work, but I'm still YOUR friend."

Silence.

> "Getting to the root of your pain can be just as hard as the past experience itself because it causes you to think back on the actual incidents(s) that took place that caused you pain in the first place."
>
> (Carliss Cole, *Pain That Heals*, 2011, p.30)

Casey decided to tell Sarah what happened that morning in the meeting with Mr. Gregory, and how what he did to her, breaking his promise, reminded her of a boss from her past who broke his promise to give her raise too, which hurt her even more.

Sarah was upset and sad when she heard this news from Casey. She decided it wasn't enough to just be Casey's best friend at work, but she should also make time to see Casey after work.

So Sarah stepped in and helped Casey take care of her mother. Sarah made sure their children and families met each other, and they all hung out together at least twice a month. Sarah also made sure that she hung out with Casey after work at least once a week. And, Sarah was right by Casey's side when she went to counseling and therapy, which was provided in their employee benefits package.

As they began to heal together, they asked Mr. Gregory if they could have Bible study once a week in Casey's office after work. Mr. Gregory agreed, and he even came to their Bible study occasionally, when he was free from any meetings and family commitments.

Casey and Sarah's friendship grew, and they promised to always be open and honest with each other so they could live in the *Pain That Heals Unforgiveness*.

* * *

Confess your faults one to another, and pray one for another, that ye may be healed. The effectual fervent prayer of a righteous man *[person]* availeth much.

James 5:16

Sarah and Casey's friendship would not have healed and blossomed if Sarah didn't care enough about Casey to change her mind about showing their boss her new Marketing Ad Project, and check on her friend instead. When we try to find out what's really wrong in our relationships, instead of letting offenses get a hold of us, we will experience the *Pain That Heals Unforgiveness* in relationships.

A friend loveth *[continually loves]* at all times…

Proverbs 17:17a

SELF-REFLECTION

Do not trivialize how you feel, no matter how others may feel about it. If it's important to you, it's important to God.**

Self-reflection is for the purpose of helping you acknowledge your past and start the healing process in your life. Trauma is something bad that happened to you—or around you—and affected you negatively.

It's important that you recognize your trauma triggers and confront them, because when you ignore them, the healing process cannot take place. When the healing process does not take place, the following problems will occur:

- Surprise behaviors/reactions that seem unrelated to the current situation (explained in detail in my first book, *Pain That Heals*)
- Major overreactions/problems with authority
- Unable to trust anyone
- Seem to always befriend people who take advantage of you

** Please do not be ashamed, embarrassed, or feel guilty for answering any of the Self-Reflection questions honestly. It is very important to be honest so you can be healed. Journaling will aid in your healing and is for your own confidentiality, which cannot be shared unless you choose to share it. A special prayer, resources about who can help, and encouraging scriptures are provided after you complete the Self-Reflection portion of this chapter.

SELF-REFLECTION – JOURNAL

What relationship trauma comes to mind after reading this chapter?

Did this relationship trauma cause patterns in your life? If so, what were the patterns in your relationships?

Do you still see those patterns in your life today? Explain.

How do you think your relationship trauma has affected you (other relationships, situations, decision making, etc.)?

Has your relationship trauma caused you to have a hard time trusting people? Explain.

Did this chapter help you understand yourself and your relationship trauma? If so, how?

Are you ready to forgive those who have caused trauma in your relationships? Why or why not?

Are you ready to forgive yourself for the wrong decisions you've made in your relationships that has caused trauma in your life? Why or why not?

If you are still struggling with unforgiveness concerning a current relationship, or in relationships from your past, here's a special prayer for you:

*Dear Heavenly Father,
I make a decision today to forgive everyone who has hurt me in any relationship from my past, and also the relationships I have right now.
Lord, I accept the truth that many of them were hurt themselves, and that's why they hurt me.*

Therefore, Lord, I forgive them, and I will no longer walk in the pain of unforgiveness in my relationships, but I will receive the Pain That Heals Unforgiveness *in all my relationships, by using my experiences to help others who are experiencing pain in their relationships right now. Thank you, Lord, for healing me.*
In Jesus' Name! Amen!

While you are praying to be healed from your pain, it is also important to work on yourself, by getting and receiving the help you need **(James 2:17)**.

You were not meant to walk through life alone. If you are still experiencing any triggers from a past relationship or even in a current relationship(s), please pray to God. If you are having a hard time praying, you can start by praying The Lord's Prayer **(Matthew 6:9 – 13)**. God will lead you from there.

Then talk to someone, like a friend or relative that you can trust. You can also contact your Pastor (Pastor's Team), a Counselor, a Therapist, or Group Therapist. These resources can be found through some employers, and also in your community, at schools and churches, and sometimes for a minimum fee or even free!

Be encouraged! God is going to work all things together for your good **(Romans 8:28)**.

Know that once you decide to forgive, the process of forgiveness begins. No matter how long it takes, God will complete his work of forgiveness in you **(Philippians 1:6)**.

Proverbs 17:17 – A friend loveth at all times, and a brother is born for adversity.

Psalm 34:17 – The righteous cry, and the Lord heareth, and delivereth them out of all their troubles.

Matthew 21:22 – And all things, whatsoever ye shall ask in prayer, believing, ye shall receive.

James 5:16 – Confess your faults one to another, that ye may be healed. The effectual fervent prayer of a righteous man availeth much.

Proverbs 11:14 – Where no counsel is the people fall: but in a multitude of counsellors there is safety.

Romans 8:28 – And we know that all things work together for good to them that love God, to them who are the called according to his purpose.

James 2:17 – Even so faith, if it hath not works, is dead, being alone.

Philippians 1:6 – Being confident of this very thing, that he which hath begun a work in you will perform it until the day of Jesus Christ.

CHAPTER 4

Pain That Heals Unforgiveness in Your Heart

Scenario 4: Margaret and Lindsey, lifetime BFFs

Margaret is in her room, and her parents are arguing. She turns up her radio. She still hears them arguing. She turns up her T.V. She still hears them arguing. Then 10 year old Margaret calls her best friend Lindsey.

Margaret: "Lindsey, my parents are arguing again! I can't take it anymore! Why did they get married in the first place? They're always arguing! I AM NEVER GETTING MARRIED WHEN I GROW UP!!!"

Lindsey tries to calm Margaret down and convince her to change her mind. But Margaret already set in her heart to NEVER GET MARRIED.

Years pass by and Margaret and Lindsey start dating guys.

Margaret meets a really nice guy named Joe, whom she's been dating for well over a year, and Joe decides to propose to Margaret in front of her parents, Lindsey, his family and friends. However, Margaret tells Joe "NO" sternly. Disappointed, Joe accepted a job offer and moved out of town.

Margaret's parents and Lindsey are upset and disappointed because of Margaret's decision. They are discussing Margaret's decision at the dining room table, while eating dinner.

Mom: "Marge, Sweetie! What is bothering you? You know as well as I do that Joe really loves you!"

Dad: "Could you just leave her alone?!"

Mom: "Leave her alone? Leave her alone?! Our daughter told a perfectly good guy who asked her to marry him NO! So NO, I'M NOT GOING TO LEAVE HER ALONE!"

Dad: "BUT THAT'S HER BUSINESS!"

Mom: "WELL IT'S MY BUSINESS TOO! I guess I'm not supposed to care who our daughter marries, because obviously you don't!"

Dad: "I DO!"

Mom: "NO YOU DON'T! ALL YOU CARE ABOUT IS YOURSELF!"

Dad: "If she wants to ruin her life, let her! It's not none of our business! So SHUT UP!"

Mom: "YOU SHUT UP!"

Margaret slams her hands on the table, stands up and yells.

> **Margaret:** "PLEASE STOP! STOP! THIS IS WHY I'M NEVER GETTING MARRIED! I DON'T WANT ME AND JOE TO END UP LIKE YOU TWO!"

Margaret leaves the dining room table and goes to her room, and Lindsey follows her.

> **Lindsey:** (calmly) "Marge, Joe is a good guy, you know."

> **Margaret:** "I know. But what if my marriage ends up like my parents?"

> **Lindsey:** "Marge, you are not your Mother, and Joe is not your Father. Besides, I want you to be in *my* wedding."

> **Margaret:** "What?! You and Luke are getting married?!"

> **Lindsey:** "Uuuuhhh...YEA! He asked me, and I ain't letting my man go!"

They both laugh.

> **Margaret:** "I can't be in your wedding Linn..."

> **Lindsey:** "What?! But you're my BEST FRIEND!"

> **Margaret:** "I told you since we were little, I'm not getting married, and I HATE marriage, so why would I be in your wedding Linn?"

Lindsey: "You are so selfish Marge! All you care about is yourself! With all that unforgiveness in your heart towards your parents! And you're taking it out on Joe! And me! And the world! You're ruining your life, Marge! And our friendship!"

Lindsey leaves crying.

* * *

> "We tend to put all of our trust in this pain rather than in the Lord of hosts, who is the healer of all pain. Even though it doesn't feel good, by ignoring it, it has become familiar; almost like nursing an old wound. When we grow accustomed to the pain, we take it into our hearts and become intimate with it. We may not like it, but it's always there; since it's been with us so long, it seems almost comfortable. We let it in every time it comes knocking on the door of our hearts. Yet, even though we know it will cause more damage, we are not willing to let go of the intimacy with the pain in our lives.
>
> We have a relationship with this pain. We have meditated on it, fed it, watered it, and taken care of it, like a mother cares for her child."
>
> (Carliss Cole, *Pain That Heals*, 2011, p.17)

> **Trust in the L**ORD **with all thine heart; and lean not unto thine own understanding. In all thy ways acknowledge him, and he shall direct thy paths.**
>
> Proverbs 3:5-6

Margaret was so hurt from seeing her parents argue all the time, to the point she was willing to not marry the person who loved her, and also disappoint her best friend.

Her pain of unforgiveness towards her parents caused her to believe that being single was better than being married, because marriage to her looked like the painful memory of what she saw from them. Her stance against marriage was strong, and she was determined that no one could change her mind.

Margaret told everyone that she needed some time away out of town for a while. She did not talk to her parents, Lindsey, and Joe for three months. But during that time she started going to church, spending personal time with God, and going to counseling.

This is when she realized that Lindsey was right, she did have the pain of unforgiveness in her heart towards her parents. So she asked God to forgive her and heal her so she could forgive her parents. And God did just that.

In the meantime, Margaret's parents realized how much their behavior damaged their daughter's whole outlook on marriage in a negative way. They realized they needed counseling.

In therapy they learned that because they both came from households with divorced parents, they never had an example of how to handle conflict in their own marriage.

However, they knew they loved each other, and were willing to do whatever was needed to have a great marriage so their daughter could begin to see marriage in a positive way.

Margaret's parents decided to renew their wedding vows after their counseling and therapy sessions. They called Margaret to tell her the great news. Margaret was so happy to hear the news about her parents renewing their wedding vows.

When she came back in town, she saw how much they really loved each other. So she decided to call Joe, and apologized to him. She also explained what happened. Then Margaret told him that she was ready to marry him. Joe was elated!

Margaret and Lindsey decided to have a double wedding.

God blessed Margaret beyond her expectations. She forgave her parents, and she experienced the joy of the *Pain That Heals Unforgiveness.*

Now unto him that is able to do exceeding abundantly above all that we ask or think, according to the power that worketh in us.

Ephesians 3:20

SELF-REFLECTION

Do not trivialize how you feel, no matter how others may feel about it. If it's important to you, it's important to God.**

Self-reflection is for the purpose of helping you acknowledge your past and start the healing process in your life. Trauma is something bad that happened to you—or around you—and affected you negatively.

It's important that you recognize your trauma triggers and confront them, because when you ignore them, the healing process cannot take place. When the healing process does not take place, the following problems will occur:

- Surprise behaviors/reactions that seem unrelated to the current situation (explained in detail in my first book, *Pain That Heals*)
- Major overreactions/problems with authority
- Unable to trust anyone
- Seem to always befriend people who take advantage of you

** Please do not be ashamed, embarrassed, or feel guilty for answering any of the Self-Reflection questions honestly. It is very important to be honest so you can be healed. Journaling will aid in your healing and is for your own confidentiality, which cannot be shared unless you choose to share it. A special prayer, resources about who can help, and encouraging scriptures are provided after you complete the Self-Reflection portion of this chapter.

S̲e̲l̲f̲-R̲e̲f̲l̲e̲c̲t̲i̲o̲n̲ – J̲o̲u̲r̲n̲a̲l̲

What traumatic heartbreak comes to mind after reading this chapter?

Did this traumatic heartbreak cause patterns in your life? If so, what were the patterns?

Do you still see those patterns in your life today? Explain.

How do you think that traumatic heartbreak experience affected you (your stance, beliefs, outlook on life, relationships, situations, decision making, etc.)?

Have your traumatic heartbreak experiences caused you to have a hard time trusting people? Explain.

Did this chapter help you understand yourself and your traumatic heartbreak more? If so, how?

Are you ready to forgive those who have caused you traumatic heartbreak? Why or why not?

Are you ready to forgive yourself for the wrong decisions you made to cause traumatic heartbreak in your life? Why or why not? *(if you were a victim, you do not have to answer this question)*

If you are still struggling with unforgiveness in your heart towards people who put you in hurtful or heartbreaking situations that you had no control over, and now you feel stuck in the memory of those situations because they are in your heart and affecting your life now, here's a special prayer for you:

Dear Heavenly Father,
I make a decision today to allow you to remove unforgiveness in my heart for those who have hurt me, and put me in hurtful situations that I had no control over.

*Lord, I accept the truth that many of the people that hurt me,
and put me in those situations, were hurting themselves.
Therefore Lord, I forgive them, and I will no longer walk in
the pain of unforgiveness in my heart, but I receive
the* Pain That Heals Unforgiveness *in my heart,
by using my experiences to help others who have the same
pain in their lives right now.
I believe I am no longer stuck in past or present situations
that are not your will for my life.
Thank you, Lord, for healing me.
In Jesus' Name! Amen!*

While you are praying to be healed from your pain, it is also important to work on yourself, by getting and receiving the help you need **(James 2:17).**

You were not meant to walk through life alone. If you are still experiencing any triggers and struggling from the memory of your past or present hurtful situations, please pray to God. If you are having a hard time praying, you can start by praying The Lord's Prayer **(Matthew 6:9 – 13).** God will lead you from there.

Then talk to someone, like a friend or relative that you can trust. You can also contact your Pastor (Pastor's Team), a Counselor, a Therapist, or Group Therapist. These resources can be found through some employers, and also in your community, at schools and churches, and sometimes for a minimum fee or even free!

Be encouraged! God is going to work all things together for your good **(Romans 8:28).**

Know that once you decide to forgive, the process of forgiveness begins. No matter how long it takes, God will complete his work of forgiveness in you **(Philippians 1:6)**.

Matthew 18:21-22 – Then came Peter to him, and said, Lord, how oft shall my brother sin against me, and I forgive him? till seven times? Jesus saith unto him, I say not unto thee, Until seven times: but, Until seventy times seven.

Psalm 34:17 – The righteous cry, and the Lord heareth, and delivereth them out of all their troubles.

Matthew 21:22 – And all things, whatsoever ye shall ask in prayer, believing, ye shall receive.

James 5:16 – Confess your faults one to another, and pray one for another, that ye may be healed. The effectual fervent prayer of a righteous man availeth much.

Proverbs 11:14 – Where no counsel is the people fall: but in a multitude of counsellors there is safety.

Romans 8:28 – And we know that all things work together for good to them that love God, to them who are the called according to his purpose.

James 2:17 – Even so faith, if it hath not works, is dead, being alone.

Philippians 1:6 – Being confident of this very thing, that he which hath begun a good work in you, will perform it until the day of Jesus Christ.

CHAPTER 5

It's Time to Forgive Yourself

Scenario 5: Pamela's guilt about her mother

Pamela wanted to be a famous singer since she was five years old. Her parents did everything they could afford to make her dream come true. While her father worked, her mother put her in beauty pageants, talent shows, and church programs.

At the age of eighteen, Pamela's father passed away after an accident on his job as a construction worker, and her mother became ill, missing her husband. Pamela had to give up her dream of becoming a famous singer to take care of her mother because she was an only child and the only one in her whole family who was willing to care for her.

Pamela resented that she was the only one, out of all her mother's family, who didn't mind taking care of her. She got a job and hired a caretaker for her mother so she could pursue her childhood dream; after all, that's what her parents wanted for her.

So Pamela headed to Hollywood, California, got an apartment, and decided to audition for every singing show that was advertised. Eventually she began to travel to different states as a first act, that's the singer who performs before the headliner comes out on stage. Pamela gained more exposure and experience in the entertainment industry.

Pamela traveled for years, while her visits to see her mother happened less often. She went from visiting her mother every other month, to three times a year, to once a year, to once every three years, to hardly seeing her at all.

Whenever Pamela did visit, she brought many beautiful gifts and plenty of money for her mother and her mother's caretaker, but her visits became shorter and shorter. Pamela's mother and her caretaker always begged Pamela to stay longer.

Eventually Pamela became a household name. She became famous. Her dream came true. She was known among the celebrities whom she used to admire as a child. She won awards, and even was asked to host an awards show. She was famous and wealthy, living the life she always wanted to live.

One day out of pure excitement Pamela decided to buy a big mansion in Hollywood, California where she was living. She wanted to surprise her mother and her mother's caretaker and move them in with her.

Pamela decided to purchase first class plane tickets for them. Then she called her mother to tell her the surprise. No one answered her mother's cell phone the first time she called, so she called again, but still there was no answer.

She looked through her phone, and noticed she received over fifteen calls from her mother's caretaker that went straight to voicemail.

Pamela called back one more time, and her mother's caretaker finally answered the phone.

>**Pamela:** "Hi! Before you start talking, I want to tell you how much I appreciate you for taking care of Mom all these years! I don't know what I would have done without you. I know I don't visit you and Mom a lot, or hardly at all, but I love you both so much! So I have a big surprise for you both! But I would like to tell Mom first. Could you put her on the phone please?"

>**Caretaker:** (very sad voice) "Pamela..."

>**Pamela:** "I know you're surprised to hear from me! But I really need to talk to my mom right now. She is going to be so happy!"

Silence on the other end.

>**Pamela:** "Hello?"

Pamela hears her mother's caretaker crying over the phone. She has never heard or even seen her cry before.

>**Caretaker:** (crying) "I'm sorry Pam...I'm so sorry...but...but....your mother...your mother...just passed...this morning...that's why I called you so much today..."

Pamela drops her phone and start screaming.

>**Pamela:** "NO! NO! NO! THIS CAN'T BE TRUE! THIS CAN'T BE TRUE! THIS CAN'T BE REAL! NO! NO! NOOOOO!"

***

Pamela's singing career went on a quick downward spiral. Pamela started drinking and taking drugs. She started getting a lot of bad press, she lost all her endorsements, and eventually stopped singing everywhere. Now she was a household name for gossip. But Pamela didn't care. She was so depressed that she missed so much time with her mother, trying to accomplish her dreams.

Pamela was angry at herself, and no matter who was nice to her, she was still mean to them, because she didn't think she deserved to be treated nicely. Pamela refused to forgive herself, so she lived a promiscuous and wild lifestyle, constantly abusing herself with drugs and alcohol. Eventually she couldn't afford all the lavish things she bought, and she ended up in rehab. Then she went from rehab to a homeless shelter.

Some of you may have addictions. Whether you're addicted to a substance, your career, a person, or pornography, it doesn't matter, because any addiction is harmful to your health: mind, soul, spirit, and body. Addictions are harmful to you as a person, and that's why God wants to set you free.

Pamela was disappointed in herself because she lost so much time with her mother while pursuing her dream. Some of you may have developed addictions because you are disappointed in yourself, like Pamela was.

Maybe you're disappointed about missing out on your children's childhood because you were busy working and trying to provide for them as a single parent. Maybe you're disappointed because you wish you would have chosen a career you love, instead of the one your parents told you to choose.

Maybe you're disappointed because when you came back from active duty, the person you thought would be waiting for you, cheated on you and married someone else, and you wish you would have married them before you even enlisted in the military.

Whatever disappointment led to your addiction, God wants you to know how much he loves you, and that he still has a plan for your life. You are not a disappointment to him.

It's time to forgive yourself for the decisions you made, that didn't bring the results you expected; whether they were mistakes, or choices made on purpose. God wants you to know that just because you made a decision which disappointed you and others, that does not make you a disappointment to him.

God wants you to know this: not only does he have a plan for your life, but he will restore those years that you feel were lost with your children, with your spouse, with your friends, and with your time. God will restore! God makes this clear in **Joel 2:25.**

And I will restore to you the years that the locust hath eaten, the cankerworm, and the caterpillar, and the palmerworm, my great army which I sent among you.

Joel 2:25

In rehab Pamela got the help she needed so she was no longer an addict, but she was still homeless, depressed, and had not forgiven herself. Then one day, she decided to go to church with some of the other people who lived in the homeless shelter. That service was the first time she heard about forgiveness.

Pamela's life changed. She received Jesus in her heart. She realized that if Jesus can forgive all of her sins, she could forgive herself. She continued going to Bible study and counseling. Her life began to blossom more and more as God gave her peace about her past. Her life continued going in a direction she never imagined was possible.

Pamela decided to enjoy the journey, and started taking college classes with plans to build her own music school. She contacted her mother's caretaker, and asked if she wanted to work as her assistant at the new music school. Pamela even gained a new family, including people from her church, her new job, and the community.

News traveled fast about Pamela building her own music school and how she was giving back to her church and community. She began to gain fans and endorsements again. Then she was asked to host an industry awards show, and surprisingly received the Humanitarian Award.

Gospel and Christian music artists began contacting Pamela, asking her to sing with them in the studio, and to be featured on their albums. As she accepted those offers, her Assistant, the former caretaker for her mother, became the Principal and Lead Administrator over her music school.

Pamela made sure she stopped in to the music school every month to spend time with her family, friends, church, and the community. She also made sure to visit her students at the school.

God did more than Pamela could have asked for, or even imagined, and he still made her name great while she represented the love and character of Jesus Christ.

> Now unto him that is able to do exceeding abundantly above all that we ask or think, according to the power that worketh *[keeps working]* in us.
>
> **Ephesians 3:20**

> ... and I will bless thee, and make thy name great; and thou shalt be a blessing.
>
> **Genesis 12:2b**

> And we know that all things work together for good to them that love God, to them who are the called according to his purpose.
>
> **Romans 8:28**

> For all the promises of God in him are yea, and in him Amen, unto the glory of God by us.
>
> **2 Corinthians 1:20**

Loved one, it's time for you to forgive yourself. Just like Pamela had to realize God's forgiveness in her life, God wants you to realize his forgiveness for you also. There is nothing you have done that God will not forgive. It's time for you to stop living in regret, and forgive yourself. When you forgive yourself, it will be easier to forgive others. The amount of love that you show towards God and to yourself will be the same amount of love you show to others.

Jesus said unto him, Thou shalt love the Lord thy God with all thy heart, and with all thy soul, and with all thy mind.

This is the first and great commandment.

And the second is like unto it, Thou shalt love thy neighbor as thyself.

Matthew 22:37-39

SELF-REFLECTION

Do not trivialize how you feel, no matter how others may feel about it. If it's important to you, it's important to God.**

Self-reflection is for the purpose of helping you acknowledge your past and start the healing process in your life. Trauma is something bad that happened to you—or around you—and affected you negatively.

It's important that you recognize your trauma triggers and confront them, because when you ignore them, the healing process cannot take place. When the healing process does not take place, the following problems will occur:

- Surprise behaviors/reactions that seem unrelated to the current situation (explained in detail in my first book, *Pain That Heals*)
- Major overreactions/problems with authority
- Unable to trust anyone
- Seem to always befriend people who take advantage of you

** Please do not be ashamed, embarrassed, or feel guilty for answering any of the Self-Reflection questions honestly. It is very important to be honest so you can be healed. Journaling will aid in your healing and is for your own confidentiality, which cannot be shared unless you choose to share it. A special prayer, resources about who can help, and encouraging scriptures are provided after you complete the Self-Reflection portion of this chapter.

SELF-REFLECTION – JOURNAL

What memory comes to mind that caused you to not forgive yourself?

Why does that memory come to mind?

Did that point of unforgiveness towards yourself cause any patterns in your life? If so, what were the patterns?

Do you still see those patterns in your life today? Explain.

How do you think not forgiving yourself has affected you (relationships, situations, decision making, etc.)?

Has not forgiving yourself caused you to mistrust people? Explain.

Did this chapter help you understand why you haven't forgiven yourself? If so, how?

Are you ready to forgive yourself? If not, why?

Do you think God has forgiven you? Why or why not?

Are you ready to receive God's forgiveness? Why or why not?

If you are still struggling with forgiving yourself, here's a special prayer for you:

Dear Heavenly Father,
I make a decision today to forgive myself
for all the decisions I've made that brought hurt
into other people's lives and into my own life.
I forgive myself for not loving you God with all of my heart,
soul, mind, and strength, which caused me to
make hurtful decisions that I regret.
I accept the truth that I hurt myself and others,
because I myself, was hurting.
Therefore Lord, I forgive myself, and I will no longer walk in
the pain of unforgiveness towards myself, but instead,
I receive the Pain That Heals Unforgiveness,
by using my experiences to help others who are experiencing
pain from not forgiving themselves right now.
Thank you, Lord, for healing me.
In Jesus' Name! Amen!

While you are praying to be healed from your pain, it is important to work on yourself, by getting and receiving the help you need **(James 2:17).**

You were not meant to walk through life alone. If you are still experiencing any triggers, are struggling from things you still regret, and are living in unforgiveness towards yourself, please pray to God. If you are having a hard time praying, you can start by praying the Lord's prayer **(Matthew 6:9 -13).** God will lead you from there.

Then you can talk to someone, like a friend or relative that you can trust. You can also contact your Pastor (Pastor's Team), a Counselor, a Therapist, or Group Therapist. These resources can be found through some employers, and also in your community, at schools and churches, and sometimes for a minimum fee or even free!

Be encouraged! God is going to work all things together for your good **(Romans 8:28)**.

Know that once you decide to forgive, the process of forgiveness begins. No matter how long it takes, God will complete his work of forgiveness in you **(Philippians 1:6)**.

Psalm 34:17 – The righteous cry, and the Lord heareth, and delivereth them out of all their troubles.

Matthew 21:22 – All things whatsoever ye shall ask in prayer, believing, ye shall receive.

James 5:16 – Confess your faults one to another, and pray one for another, that ye may be healed. The effectual fervent prayer of a righteous man availeth much."

Proverbs 11:14 – Where no counsel is, the people fall: but in a multitude of counsellors there is safety."

Romans 8:28 – And we know that all things work together for good to them that love God, to them who are the called according to his purpose.

James 2:17 – Even so faith, if it hath not works, is dead, being alone.

Philippians 1:6 – Being confident of this very thing, that he which hath begun a good work in you will perform it until the day of Jesus Christ.

YOU ARE FORGIVEN!!!!

CHAPTER 6

It's Time to Forgive God

Getting to the Root of Unforgiveness

This is the last layer in the onion of unforgiveness that you have to peel off. I know reading this book has been like peeling an onion. For many of you, it has brought tears to your eyes. Reading each scenario should cause you to think about your own life and then honestly respond to the Self-Reflection questions towards the end of each chapter. Just know that while you are peeling this onion, while you may be crying, God is healing your unforgiving heart. But before you can completely heal, you must know, it's time to forgive God.

Yes, God your Creator. God the Father. God who loves you so much that he sent his son Jesus to die on the cross for your sins, so that you can live with him forever. Yes, God! That same God! The Only One True Living, Loving God. It's time for you to forgive God.

There's no scenario I can give you for having unforgiveness towards God, because many of us tend to blame God for everything that causes us pain, ranging from our childhood disappointments to our unexpected heartbreaks as an adult. The problem is, many of us don't believe we have unforgiveness in our hearts towards God, because we still pray, and still go to church regularly, but that doesn't exempt us from having unforgiveness towards God.

I had unforgiveness towards God. He allowed me to be raped and molested as an innocent child, yet I had to go to church and hear how good God was to me. That was confusing to me.

I had unforgiveness towards God because of what I saw my mother go through when I was a child. She was a single parent who worked three jobs. I remember we used to walk to church. Many times some of the people who were members of the same church, and were considered my mother's "friends" drove right past us, while Mother, my two siblings and I walked home from church. Many of them never offered us, my struggling mother and her three children, a ride home after church.

Even worse, I remember standing beside her when she asked for a ride home; many of those same members who we saw every Sunday, would say to my mother without conviction, compassion, or concern, "No, I'm not going that way."

I had unforgiveness in my heart towards God when my mother passed away. I went on a 40 day, liquid-only fast, while praying for her body to be healed, only for her to pass away right after I came off of that fast. Then I had to be in charge of arranging her funeral, since she only told me exactly how she wanted her funeral to be.

I had unforgiveness in my heart when my dad passed. Even though he lived longer than my mother, he was still the only parent I had left. The pain felt unbearable! What was God doing to me?

I had unforgiveness in my heart towards God, when no matter how I tried to please God and people, some people still misunderstood me and/or mistreated me.

By now you may be wondering, how did I know that I had unforgiveness towards God? You may also wonder; how can you know whether you have unforgiveness towards God?

There are several ways you can know if you have unforgiveness towards God.

You will know you have unforgiveness towards God when you blame God for everything.

You will know you have unforgiveness towards God when you stop having faith in him, and start leaning to your own understanding, because your pain has caused you to no longer trust God, even though **Proverbs 3:5** tells us to do so.

Trust in the LORD with all thine heart; and lean not unto thine own understanding.

Proverbs 3:5

You will know you have unforgiveness towards God when you stop acknowledging him and following him, even though **Proverbs 3:6** tells us to do so.

In all thy ways acknowledge him, and he shall direct thy paths.

Proverbs 3:6

You will know you have unforgiveness towards God when you stop loving him. And when you stop loving him, you will stop obeying him.

> **Jesus said uno him, Thou shalt love the Lord thy God with all thy heart, and with all thy soul, and with all thy mind. This is the first and great commandment.**
>
> **Matthew 22:37-38**

> **If ye love me, keep my commandments.**
>
> **John 14:15**

You will know you have unforgiveness towards God when you begin to doubt his very existence, because of the painful experiences in your life, and the pain you have seen others go through.

Then you will begin to seek out other things, because you think the answer to your problems, and the problems of the world, is found somewhere else. You will start to believe everything you want in the world, can be found in those things, even though **Matthew 6:33** clearly says different.

> **But seek ye first the kingdom of God, and his righteousness; and all these things shall be added unto you.**
>
> **Matthew 6:33**

You will know you have unforgiveness towards God, when you refuse to forgive yourself and others, because you have allowed your pain to have first place in your life, instead of God's Word, which tells us that Jesus wants us to have a forgiving heart.

Then came Peter to him, and said, Lord, how oft shall my brother sin against me, and I forgive him? till seven times? Jesus saith unto him, I say not unto thee, Until seven times: but, Until seventy times seven.

Matthew 18:21-22

And, you'll know you have unforgiveness in your heart towards God when you completely turn away from God. This is called "backsliding", which is renouncing God's ways, because you believe his ways don't work for you, and instead, you decide to do things your own way.

The backslider in heart shall be filled with his own ways…

Proverbs 14:14a

The good news is, if you have unforgiveness in your heart towards God—even if you've done all of these things—he doesn't have unforgiveness in his heart towards you. Even though you may have turned completely away from God and backslid, he hasn't turned away from you. And he never will. God loves you always and forever.

…for he hath said, I will never leave thee, nor forsake thee.
Hebrews 13:5b

Turn, O backsliding children, saith the LORD; for I am married unto you…
Jeremiah 3:14a

Be strong and of a good courage, fear not, nor be afraid of them: for the LORD thy God, he it is that doth go with thee; he will not fail thee, nor forsake thee.
Deuteronomy 31:6

...and, lo, I am with you always, even unto the end of the world. Amen.

Matthew 28:20b

...Yea, I have loved thee with an everlasting love: therefore with lovingkindness have I drawn thee.

Jeremiah 31:3b

I did all of those things when I had an unforgiving heart towards God. I thank God for his lovingkindness towards me, which gave me the ability to forgive him, myself, and others. I know God can, and will, do the same for you.

I thank God for his patience towards me. I grew up with such a false mindset concerning God, which is why I had unforgiveness in my heart towards him. My young mind believed that if you went to church faithfully, all your struggles in life would end. I often wondered as a child, why my mother's struggles never ended.

I grew up believing that being a Christian meant I wasn't supposed to go through a lot. I thought if you struggled too long, you must be doing something wrong.

It often felt like the people who "seemed" as if they had it all together, because they had more material things, were the "Chosen Ones" by God; they were often treated better and considered the "Holier Ones" because their tithes and offerings also reflected that God loved them more.

I didn't know how to separate God's pure unconditional love towards my mother, my siblings, and me, from people's fickle conditional love towards us. I thought they were the same, which gave me even more of a reason to have unforgiveness in my heart towards God.

However, as I came into my own personal relationship with Jesus Christ and studied the Word of God for myself, I realized many of the things in church that I saw, was taught, and believed, were not true.

I began to see in God's Word that there were people in the Bible who went through terrible situations, and, like my mother, didn't do anything wrong, but found themselves in it.

Job had everything taken away from him and found himself in a terribly painful situation, but he still made the right choice (I encourage you to read the whole book of Job when you have time).

The Job arose, and rent his mantle, and shaved his head, and fell down upon the ground, and worshipped,

And said, Naked came I out of my mother's womb, and naked shall I return thither: the LORD gave, and the LORD hath taken away; blessed be the name of the LORD.

In all this Job sinned not, nor charged God foolishly.

Job 1:20-22

Although Job made the right choice, there are times while in the midst of our own suffering, we make wrong choices. When this happens, I believe it's important for us to admit some of our unforgiveness towards God has to do with those wrong choices we made.

We must realize that bad things happen. Sometimes it's because of our own choices that could have been avoided; we definitely had control over our behavior in those situations. God will let us know he is not pleased with the bad choices we made. For example, 2 Samuel chapter 11 tells the story of King David and Bathsheba. David slept with Bathsheba, who was married to Uriah, and then plotted to have Uriah killed when she became pregnant (read the complete story when you have time).

> **...But the thing that David had done displeased the LORD.**
> **2 Samuel 11:27b**

However, in each of those Bible stories, God ultimately showed his unconditional love towards both Job and David. He blessed Job with more than what he had originally, and still called David a man after his own heart. Knowing God loves us unconditionally, whether we make the right or wrong choice, is evidence that God deserves to be forgiven.

> **...also the LORD gave Job twice as much as he had before.**
> **Job 42:10b**

> **...the LORD hath sought him a man after his own heart *[which was David]*...**
> **1 Samuel 13:14a**

Jesus understands what we're going through, and he's personally touched by our pain. He doesn't take it lightly, that's why he endured even greater pain HIMSELF.

For we have not an high priest which cannot be touched with the feeling of our infirmities; but was in all points tempted like as we are, yet without sin.

Hebrews 4:15

He is despised and rejected of men; a man of sorrows, and acquainted with grief: and we hid as it were our faces from him; he was despised, and we esteemed him not.

Surely he hath borne our griefs, and carried our sorrows: yet we did esteem him stricken, smitten of God, and afflicted.

But he was wounded for our transgressions, he was bruised for our iniquities: the chastisement of our peace was upon him; and with his stripes we are healed.

Isaiah 53:3-5

If you are ready to forgive God, you may be wondering, how do you forgive God?

I don't have steps to tell you what to do. I don't have a specific plan for you to follow. All I have is the Word of God, which is the Bible. When you believe what the Bible says, you are believing God the Father, God the son Jesus, and God the Holy Spirit. All of them are one.

In the beginning was the Word *[Jesus]*, and the Word was with God, and the Word was God.

John 1:1

And the Word *[Jesus]* was made flesh, and dwelt among us...

John 1:14a

And I will put my spirit within you, and cause you to walk in my statutes, and ye shall keep my judgements, and do them.

Ezekiel 36:27

For there are three that bear record in heaven, the Father, the Word *[Jesus]* , and the Holy Ghost: and these three are one.

1 John 5:7

You may not fully understand it right now, but if you are willing and ready to forgive him, that's a start. Begin by believing in him. To believe in him, is to believe in the Word of God (the Bible).

I'm not going to lie and tell you that this is going to be easy, because it's not; especially when what you believe is totally opposite of what you see, feel, and have gone through. But you must hold on and believe his Word no matter what!

Let me warn you, it's going to take a lot of work.

…faith without works is dead…

James 2:26b

So what work is needed to not only forgive God, but walk in that forgiveness? It is to *believe, accept,* and *receive.*

Look, I know some of you really feel that you already believe his Word. I understand, I felt the same way. But God showed me that I really didn't believe his Word. He took me a step further and showed me what it really means to believe in his Word. When I did it *his* way, I was able to forgive God, myself, and others.

God told me: to **believe** his Word, is to **accept** his Word. When you **accept** his Word, that's when you actually **receive** his Word. **Receive means to take in**, so that means the Word goes into your heart and heals you of all unforgiveness you have toward God, yourself, and others.

For example: You go to your doctor because you **believe** what he says about your health. When you **believe** what the doctor says, you **accept** the prescription he gives you. When you **accept** that prescription, you go to the store to buy and **receive** the medicine from the pharmacy. Then you bring the medicine home to take and **receive** it into your body. When you **receive** the medicine in your body, that's when your body begins to heal. And, just like when you take medicine, your personal healing (forgiving God, yourself, and others) will happen over the process of time. So don't rush your healing. Just be consistent in doing the work, by **believing, accepting, and receiving** God's Word.

In my own life, I had to take the medicine of **Romans 8:28** for years when it came to being a victim of rape and molestation as a child. It was just hard for me to believe this scripture.

And we know that all things work together for good to them that love God, to them who are the called according to his purpose.

Romans 8:28

I had to **believe, accept, and receive,** that being molested and raped (even though it wasn't good and wasn't of God, but an attack from Satan), would somehow eventually work together for my good.

That was hard. I read this scripture for years thinking about what I went through as a child; angry, upset, unforgiving, and feeling like my childhood was stolen from me. I was upset! **Romans 8:28** was some nasty medicine for me. A lot of times medicine tastes nasty, even though it's good for you.

That's the way I felt about **Romans 8:28**, it was nasty. But as I continued to read it, meditate on it, and study it, I began to **believe, accept, and receive** it. That's when I started to heal.

God used me to speak to hundreds of women at conferences through my writings. He used me to help bring healing to their lives in the same areas where I had been traumatized, which brought even more healing to my life! **Romans 8:28** became alive in me! I was healed from my childhood trauma.

Today the memory of being raped and molested doesn't even sting anymore. It's just a memory. I forgave the people who raped and molested me as well. I'm amazed at the miracle working power of God. He can work wonders in our lives if we just give him a chance to heal us, by **believing, accepting, and receiving the healing medicine of his Word.**

Romans 8:28 and other scriptures are medicines I continue to take for each and every situation in my life. The Word of God is medicine that will bring healing to your spirit, mind, body, and soul. Take your daily dose and you will be healed!

Always remember that no matter what you have been through, and whatever you are going through now, God wants you to **believe, accept**, and **receive** his Word concerning your situation, so he can heal you of unforgiveness towards him, yourself, and others.

The book of Genesis in the Bible clearly tells us that the origin of our pain is sin. Every painful experience is a result of the fall of Adam and Eve. When sin came into this world, so did pain (explained more in my first book, *Pain That Heals*, chapter three, "The Origin of Pain").

God wants you to **believe, accept,** and **receive** how much he loves you. He also wants you to **believe, accept,** and **receive** his Son Jesus into your heart.

For God so loved the world, that he gave his only begotten Son, that whosoever believeth in him should not perish, but have everlasting life.

John 3:16

God wants you to **believe, accept**, and **receive** that he knows and understands every pain of unforgiveness in your past, and whatever pain you have right now.

Surely he hath borne our griefs, and carried our sorrows: yet we did esteem him stricken, smitten of God, and afflicted. But he was wounded for our transgressions, he was bruised for our iniquities: the chastisement of our peace was upon him; and with his stripes we are healed.

Isaiah 53:4-5

For we have not an high priest which cannot be touched with the feeling of our infirmities; but was in all points tempted like as we are, yet without sin.

Hebrews 4:15

God wants you to **believe, accept**, and **receive**, that no matter what you are going through, he is with you.

Fear thou not; for I am with thee: be not dismayed; for I am thy God: I will strengthen thee; yea, I will help thee; yea, I will uphold thee with the right hand of my righteousness.

Isaiah 41:10

God wants you to **believe, accept**, and **receive,** that he will not lie to you.

God is not a man, that he should lie; neither the son of man, that he should repent: hath he said, and shall he not do it? or hath he spoken, and shall he not make it good?

Numbers 23:19

For all the promises of God in him are yea, and in him Amen, unto the glory of God by us.

2 Corinthians 1:20

God wants you to **believe, accept**, and **receive** that he truly loves you.

But God commendeth *[continually demonstrates]* his love toward us, in that, while we were yet sinners, Christ died for us.

Romans 5:8

SELF-REFLECTION

Do not trivialize how you feel, no matter how others may feel about it. If it's important to you, it's important to God.**

Self-reflection is for the purpose of helping you acknowledge your past and start the healing process in your life. Trauma is something bad that happened to you—or around you—and affected you negatively.

It's important that you recognize your trauma triggers and confront them, because when you ignore them, the healing process cannot take place. When the healing process does not take place, the following problems will occur:

- Surprise behaviors/reactions that seem unrelated to the current situation (explained in detail in my first book, *Pain That Heals*)
- Major overreactions/problems with authority
- Unable to trust anyone
- Seem to always befriend people who take advantage of you

** Please do not be ashamed, embarrassed, or feel guilty for answering any of the Self-Reflection questions honestly. It is very important to be honest so you can be healed. Journaling will aid in your healing and is for your own confidentiality, which cannot be shared unless you choose to share it. A special prayer, resources about who can help, and encouraging scriptures are provided after you complete the Self-Reflection portion of this chapter.

S<small>ELF</small>-R<small>EFLECTION</small> – J<small>OURNAL</small>

What memory comes to mind concerning your unforgiveness toward God?

Did this memory of your unforgiveness toward God cause a pattern in your life? If so, what was the pattern?

Do you still see those patterns in your life? Explain.

How do you think your unforgiveness towards God has affected you (your relationships, situations, decision making, etc.)?

Has your unforgiveness toward God caused you to have a hard time trusting people? Explain.

Did reading this chapter help you understand yourself and why you have unforgiveness toward God? If so, how?

Are you ready to forgive God? Why or why not?

Are you ready to forgive those who caused the trauma which brought you to a place of unforgiveness toward God?

Are you ready to forgive yourself for making wrong decisions that may have caused trauma in your life, bringing you to a place of unforgiveness toward God? Why or why not?

You may have heard the phrase "God Is Love." Do you believe that? Why or why not?

Do you believe God loves you? Why or why not?

If you are still having a hard time forgiving God and believing that God loves you, here's a special prayer for you:

*Dear Heavenly Father,
I make a decision today to forgive you
for allowing me to endure painful experiences in my past that
I wish I didn't have to go through.
I forgive you for allowing me to endure some painful things
right now, even though I just don't want to go through it.
Lord, I believe, accept, and receive your Word that
everything I go through is working for my good,
even when it hurts.
I only want your will to be done in my life.
Therefore, Lord, I forgive you, and I will no longer walk in
the pain of unforgiveness toward your will for my life.
I receive the* Pain That Heals Unforgiveness *toward you God,
by using my own pain to help others
who are experiencing the pain of unforgiveness
toward you in their lives right now.
Thank you, Lord for healing me.
In Jesus' Name! Amen.*

While you are praying to be healed from your pain, it is important to work on yourself, by getting and receiving the help you need **(James 2:17)**.

You were not meant to walk through life alone. If you are still experiencing triggers and struggling with unforgiveness toward God, please keep talking to God. If you are having a hard time praying, you can start by praying The Lord's Prayer **(Matthew 6:9-13).** God will help you from there.

Then talk to someone, like a friend or relative you can trust. You can also contact your Pastor (Pastor's Team), a Counselor, a Therapist, Group Therapist. These resources can sometimes be found through Employers, your communities, schools, and churches, sometimes for a minimum fee or free!

Be encouraged! God is working all things together for your good **(Romans 8:28).**

Know that once you decide to forgive, the process of forgiveness begins. No matter how long it takes, God will complete his work of forgiveness in you **(Philippians 1:6).**

Psalm 34:17 – The righteous cry, and the Lord heareth, and delivereth them out of all their troubles.

Matthew 21:22 – And all things, whatsoever ye shall ask in prayer, believing, ye shall receive.

James 5:16 – Confess your faults one to another, and pray one for another, that ye may be healed. The effectual fervent prayer of a righteous man availeth much.

Proverbs 11:14 – Where no counsel is, the people fall: but in the multitude of counsellors there is safety.

Romans 8:28 – And we know that all things work together for good to them that love God, to them who are the called according to his purpose.

James 2:17 – Even faith, if it hath not works, is dead, being alone.

Philippians 1:6 – Being confident of this very thing, that he which hath begun a good work in you will perform it until the day of Jesus Christ.

CHAPTER 7

You Are Forgiven!

Dealing With the Scribes and Pharisees / Your Haters

Even after reading this far, there are some of you who are still struggling to forgive yourself. How do I know? The Lord specifically told me to implement this chapter for you. Again, I say specifically for YOU!

The Lord told me that some of you all are having a hard time forgiving yourself, not because you haven't forgiven others or God, but because you are dealing with the Scribes and Pharisees, your haters, who keep throwing your past up in your face.

They don't want you to move on and be free. They want you to remember the wrong you've done to them and others, no matter how many times you've apologized. When people do this, they are condemning you and unfortunately, they want you to live in condemnation.

To live in condemnation means to live with a guilty conscience, to live with a continual sense of regret for the wrong choices you've made. This was explained in Chapter 5, when Pamela condemned herself for not being there to take care of her mother who passed while she pursued her career. But by the end of the chapter Pamela received the love and redemption power of the cross through Jesus Christ. She received the peace of God to forgive herself, then God restored her, and her life became better than ever.

It's so important for you to know that condemnation is not of God. Whenever you're feeling condemned, recognize that feeling comes from Satan himself. He doesn't want you to know how much God loves you and that God has forgiven you.

The woman caught in adultery experienced the same thing. The Scribes and Pharisees condemned her **(John 8:3-11)**.

"And the scribes and Pharisees brought unto him a woman taken in adultery; and when they had set her in the midst,

They say unto him, Master, this woman was taken in adultery, in the very act.

Now Moses in the law commanded us, that such should be stoned: but what sayest thou?
This they said, tempting him, that they might have to accuse him. But Jesus stooped down, and with his finger wrote on the ground, as though he heard them not.

So when they continued asking him, he lifted up himself, and said unto them, He that is without sin among you, let him first cast a stone at her.

And again he stooped down, and wrote on the ground.

And they which heard it, being convicted by their own conscience, went out one by one, beginning at the eldest, even unto the last: and Jesus was left alone, and the woman standing in the midst.

When Jesus had lifted up himself, and saw none but the woman, he said unto her, Woman, where are those thine accusers? hath no man condemned thee?

She said, No man, Lord. And Jesus said unto her, Neither do I condemn thee: go, and sin no more."

God made it clear to the woman caught in adultery that he didn't condemn her for her act of adultery, he forgave her. He also made it clear that no one has the right to condemn, because we all have sinned.

For all have sinned, and come short of the glory of God.
Romans 3:23

Now, God will convict us. That means God will let us know that we have done something wrong. Oftentimes, God will use people in our lives to call out a wrong we have committed, especially if we continue to do it. This is necessary because Jesus loves us.

For whom the Lord loveth he chasteneth *[disciplines]*...
Hebrews 12:6a

However, if someone is taunting you, constantly pointing the finger and reminding you of your sins, that is not of God. God does not approve of that behavior. God sent Jesus so we can be saved and forgiven of our sins, not to condemn us.

For God sent not his Son into the world to condemn the world; but that the world through him might be saved.
John 3:17

But what if it seems like the Scribes, Pharisees, and haters in your life, won't stop; even though you have forgiven God, others, and yourself, and have done everything you read in this book up to this point?

That's when you have to cast your cares on God.

Casting all you care upon him *[keep giving all your cares to him]*; **for he careth** *[continually cares]* **for you.**

1 Peter 5:7

It is so important that we cast our cares on God, because if we don't, we will find ourselves treating them (Scribes, Pharisees, and haters) the same way they treat us; arguing with them and condemning them, instead of loving them, praying for them, and doing good towards them.

But I say unto you, Love your enemies, bless them that curse you, do good to them that hate you, and pray for them which despitefully use you, and persecute you.

Mathew 5:44

My point is, Jesus still loved and died for the very people that talked about him, condemned him, and even crucified him.

For God so loved the world *[that includes Scribes, Pharisees, and haters]*, **that he gave his only begotten Son, that whosoever believeth in him should not perish, but have everlasting life.**

John 3:16

You may not want to read or hear this, but God's solution to every Scribe, Pharisee, and hater in your life is to still love them. **John 3:16** begins with "For God so loved the world". That means GOD LOVES ALL PEOPLE! No matter who we are, or what we've done, God loves and forgives us ALL.

So I conclude this chapter by encouraging you to realize you have been forgiven, in spite of what your Scribes, Pharisees, and haters are saying about you. I also encourage you to ask God to help you love them, because your love and forgiveness towards them will bring healing to you, and it will also bring healing to them. LOVE IS THE KEY!

And now abideth *[continually abides]* faith, hope, charity *[love]*, these three; but the greatest of these is charity *[love]*.
1 Corinthians 13:13

SELF-REFLECTION

Do not trivialize how you feel, no matter how others may feel about it. If it's important to you, it's important to God.**

Self-reflection is for the purpose of helping you acknowledge your past and start the healing process in your life. Trauma is something bad that happened to you—or around you—and affected you negatively.

It's important that you recognize your trauma triggers and confront them, because when you ignore them, the healing process cannot take place. When the healing process does not take place, the following problems will occur:

- Surprise behaviors/reactions that seem unrelated to the current situation (explained in detail in my first book, *Pain That Heals*)
- Major overreactions/problems with authority
- Unable to trust anyone
- Seem to always befriend people who take advantage of you

** Please do not be ashamed, embarrassed, or feel guilty for answering any of the Self-Reflection questions honestly. It is very important to be honest so you can be healed. Journaling will aid in your healing and is for your own confidentiality, which cannot be shared unless you choose to share it. A special prayer, resources about who can help, and encouraging scriptures are provided after you complete the Self-Reflection portion of this chapter.

SELF-REFLECTION – JOURNAL

What comes to mind after reading this chapter? Why?

Did the memory of what you've gone through with your Scribes, Pharisees, and haters cause any patterns in your life? If so, what patterns were caused?

Do you still see those patterns in your life today? Explain.

How do you think your Scribes, Pharisees, and haters have affected you (relationships, situations, decision making, etc.)?

Have your Scribes, Pharisees, and haters caused you to have a hard time trusting people? Explain.

Did reading this chapter help you understand yourself more concerning your Scribes, Pharisees, and haters? If so, how?

Are you ready to forgive your Scribes, Pharisees, and haters? Why or why not?

Are you ready to ask God to help you show love to your Scribes, Pharisees, and haters? Why or why not?

If you are still struggling with people who are constantly reminding you of your past, if you have a hard time forgiving your Scribes, Pharisees, and haters, and you don't want to show love to them, here's a special prayer for you:

Dear Heavenly Father,
I make a decision today to forgive and love
the Scribes, Pharisees, and haters (bullies) in my life,
and to forgive everyone who has hurt me in the past,
and even those who are hurting me now
with the constant reminders of my past mistakes and sins.
I forgive them for making it hard for me to
even forgive myself.

*I accept the truth that many of them are hurting and still have not forgiven You, themselves, or others, in their own lives, and that's why they continue to hurt me.
Therefore, I forgive them, and I will no longer walk in the pain of unforgiveness concerning anyone who brings up my past.
I receive the* Pain That Heals Unforgiveness *for those who are unforgiving about my past.
I will use my experiences to help others who are experiencing pain from anyone who keeps bringing up their past.
Thank you, Lord, for healing me!
In Jesus' Name! Amen!*

While you are praying to be healed from your pain, it is also important to work on yourself, by getting and receiving the help you need **(James 2:17).**

You were not meant to walk through life alone. If you are experiencing any triggers and struggle with people that are unforgiving and constantly bring up your past, please pray to God. If you are having a hard time praying, you can start by praying The Lord's Prayer **(Matthew 6:9–13)**. God will lead you from there.

Then talk to someone, like a friend or relative you can trust. You can also contact your Pastor (Pastor's Team), a Counselor, a Therapist, or Group Therapist. These resources can be found through some employers, and also in your community, at schools and churches, and sometimes for a minimum fee or even free!

Be encouraged. God is working all things together for your good **(Romans 8:28).**

Know that once you decide to forgive, the process of forgiveness begins. No matter how long it takes, God will complete his work of forgiveness in you **(Philippians 1:6).**

Philippians 3:13-14 – Brethren, I count not myself to have apprehended: but this one thing I do, forgetting those things which are behind, and reaching forth unto those things which are before, I press toward the mark for the prize of the high calling of God in Christ Jesus.

2 Corinthians 5:17 – Therefore if any man be in Christ, he is a new creature: old things are passed away; behold, all things are become new.

Proverbs 34:17 – The righteous cry, and the Lord heareth, and delivereth them out of all their troubles.

Matthew 21:22 – And all things, whatsoever ye shall ask in prayer, believing, ye shall receive.

James 5:16 – Confess your faults one to another, and pray one for another, that ye may be healed. The effectual fervent prayer of a righteous man availeth much.

Proverbs 11:14 – Where no counsel is, the people fall: but in the multitude of counsellors there is safety.

Romans 8:28 – And we know that all things work together for good to them that love God, to them who are the called according to his purpose.

James 2:17 – Even so faith, if it hath not works, is dead, being alone.

Philippians 1:6 – Being confident of this very thing, that he which hath begun a work in you will perform it until the day of Jesus Christ.

CHAPTER 8

You Are Healed!

You Are an Overcomer!

Now, before I continue, I don't want you to have the impression that the pain of unforgiveness will not come knocking at the door of your life. As long as we exist on this earth, pain will continue to be a part of our lives. We will be tried and tempted to walk in the pain of unforgiveness, but if you've read this far, you have allowed God to begin the healing process in you. Even though this process has begun, the Word of God already declares that YOU ARE HEALED! AMEN! That means you have experienced the *Pain That Heals Unforgiveness*. Please do not allow the enemy to steal it from you.

How do you know you are an overcomer? The first step was reading this book, and then doing everything the Lord gave me to teach you, according to the Word of God. That's when you know that you are truly an Overcomer.

I want to clarify this, because there were times in my life when I thought I overcame the pain of unforgiveness, but I found myself drinking alcohol to numb the pain. I found myself going out to clubs and being promiscuous to numb the pain of rejection and abuse, thinking that I'm actually going to find love and approval from someone, or something else. This behavior clearly showed me that I had not overcome the pain of unforgiveness.

It was only when I received Jesus into my heart and life, and started ***believing, accepting, and receiving*** the Word of God, that I truly became an overcomer.

So now, when I go through hard times in life, I've learned (and still am learning) to trust God by ***believing, accepting, and receiving*** his Word.

These things I have spoken unto you, that in me ye might have peace. In the world ye shall have tribulation: but be of good cheer; I have overcome the world.

John 16:33

Since Jesus overcame the world, with him in our lives, we can and will overcome the world too!

> **For whatsoever is born of God overcometh the world: and this is the victory that overcometh the world, even our faith.**
>
> **I John 5:4**

I believe you can come to a place in life where pain no longer causes you to walk in unforgiveness towards, God, yourself, and others.

I do believe the more you tap into the love of God on a daily basis, you will dispense His love towards other people, no matter how they treat you.

I'm not saying that you will become invincible where no person or situation will ever hurt or affect you again. But I do believe it doesn't have to pull you back into living with the pain of unforgiveness.

> **Be not overcome of evil, but overcome evil with good.**
>
> **Romans 12:21**

YOU ARE AN OVERCOMER!!!!

Ye are of God, little children, and have overcome them: because greater is he that is in you, than he that is in the world.

1 John 4:4

Who is he that overcometh the world, but he that believeth that Jesus is the Son of God?

1 John 5:5

He that overcometh, the same shall be clothed in white raiment; and I will not blot out his name out of the book of life, but I will confess his name before my Father, and before his angels.

Revelation 3:5

SELF-REFLECTION

Do not trivialize how you feel, no matter how others feel about it. If it's important to you, it's important to God.**

Self-reflection is for the purpose of helping you acknowledge your past and start the healing process in your life. Trauma is something bad that happened to you—or around you—and affected you negatively.

It's important that you recognize your trauma triggers and confront them, because when you ignore them, the healing process cannot take place. When the healing process does not take place, the following problems will occur:

- Surprise behaviors/reactions that seem unrelated to the current situation (explained in detail in my first book, *Pain That Heals*)
- Major overreactions/problems with authority
- Unable to trust anyone
- Seem to always befriend people who take advantage of you

** Please do not be ashamed, embarrassed, or feel guilty for answering any of the Self-Reflection questions honestly. It is very important to be honest so you can be healed. Journaling will aid in your healing and is for your own confidentiality, which cannot be shared unless you choose to share it. A special prayer, resources about who can help, and encouraging scriptures are provided after you complete the Self-Reflection portion of this chapter.

S<small>ELF</small>-R<small>EFLECTION</small> – J<small>OURNAL</small>

What trauma remains in your life that you still need to overcome?

How has that remaining trauma affected you (relationships, situations, decision making, etc.)?

Has your remaining trauma made it hard for you to trust people? Explain.

Did reading this chapter help you understand the importance of overcoming your trauma? Explain.

Are you ready to overcome? Why or why not?

Do you believe you are an overcomer? Why or why not?

If you find yourself still struggling to overcome unforgiveness, here's a special prayer for you:

*Dear Heavenly Father,
I make the decision today to be an overcomer and forgive everyone who has hurt me, from my past up until today.
I understand the truth that many of the people who hurt me and the situations I've been in, have affected me to the point where it felt impossible to overcome.
I accept the truth that I am a flawed human being,
and I don't always understand you Lord,
but I receive the truth of your Word,
that I am an Overcomer!
I am still making the decision to forgive everyone,
in every situation.
I forgive you Lord, and myself.
Today I choose to no longer walk in the pain of unforgiveness because I receive the* Pain That Heals Unforgiveness
*in every area of my life.
I will use my experiences to help others who are experiencing the same pain right now.
Thank you, Lord, for healing me!
In Jesus' Name! Amen!*

While you are praying to be healed from your pain, it is also important to work on yourself, by getting and receiving the help you need **(James 2:17).**

You were not meant to walk through life alone. If you find yourself experiencing triggers and struggling with unforgiveness in any area of your life, please pray to God. If you are having a hard time praying, you can start by praying The Lord's Prayer **(Matthew 6:9-13).** God will lead you from there.

Then talk to someone, like a friend or relative that you can trust. You can also contact your Pastor (Pastors Team), a Counselor, a Therapist, or Group Therapist. These resources can be found through some employers, and also in your community, at schools and churches, and sometimes for a minimum fee or even free!

Be encouraged! God is working all things together for your good **(Romans 8:28).**

Know that once you decide to forgive, the process of forgiveness begins. No matter how long it takes, God will complete his work of forgiveness in you **(Philippians 1:6).**

Romans 12:21 – Be not overcome of evil, but overcome evil with good.

Proverbs 34:17 – The righteous cry, and the Lord heareth, and delivereth them out of all their troubles.

Matthew 21:22 – And all things, whatsoever ye shall ask in prayer, believing, ye shall receive.

James 5:16 – Confess your faults one to another, and pray one for another, that ye may be healed. The effectual fervent prayer of a righteous man availeth much.

Proverbs 11:14 – Where no counsel is, the people fall: but in the multitude of counsellors there is safety.

Romans 8:28 – And we know that all things work together for good to them that love God, to them who are the called according to his purpose.

James 2:17 – Even so faith, if it hath not works, is dead, being alone.

Philippians 1:6 – Being confident of this very thing, that he which hath begun a good work in you will perform it until the day of Jesus Christ.

CHAPTER 9

A New Beginning

The Benefits of Forgiveness and Freedom

Now that you no longer walk in the pain of unforgiveness, it's important that you know and understand the Benefits of Forgiveness.

The Lord put on my heart to implement this chapter, because there will be some challenges that tempt you to have a valid reason to walk in unforgiveness. You still have to make the right choice and forgive anyway, because there are actual benefits to having a forgiving heart and living in freedom.

You need to know that all of the hurt, pain, and suffering that you go through in this life, tempting you to walk in unforgiveness, is not in vain. When you do it God's way, and forgive, the glory of God will be revealed in you. This is just one of the benefits of forgiveness found in **Romans 8:18.**

For I reckon that the sufferings of this present time are not worthy to be compared with the glory which shall be revealed in us.
Romans 8:18

Another benefit of forgiveness is that when we forgive others, God will forgive us. This is found in **Matthew 6:15** and **Mark 11:25**.

But if you forgive not men their trespasses, neither will your Father forgive your trespasses.
Matthew 6:15

And when ye stand praying, forgive, if ye have ought against any: that your Father also which is in heaven may forgive you your trespasses.
Mark 11:25

Another benefit of forgiveness is that when we confess our sins, God continually forgives us for our sins. This reassures us that we will live in heaven with him one day. This is found in **1 John 1:9**.

If we confess our sins, he is faithful and just to forgive us our sins, and to cleanse us from all unrighteousness.

1 John 1:9

Another benefit of forgiveness is we also receive the mercy of God. **Hebrews 8:12** and **Matthew 5:7** tell us this.

For I will be merciful to their unrighteousness, and their sins and their iniquities will I remember no more.

Hebrews 8:12

Blessed are the merciful: for they shall obtain mercy.

Matthew 5:7

Another benefit of forgiveness is that it causes others to fear (respect) you. God is feared (respected) because of his forgiveness toward us. This is found in **Psalm 130:4.**

But there is forgiveness with thee, that thou mayest be feared *[respected]*.

Psalm 130:4

Another benefit of forgiveness is you become NEW! Each time you ask for forgiveness, and each time you forgive someone else, you get a New Beginning! This is found in **2 Corinthians 5:17** and **Isaiah 43: 18-19.**

Therefore if any man be in Christ, he is a new creature: old things are passed away; behold, all things are become new.

2 Corinthians 5:17

Remember ye not the former things, neither consider the things of old. Behold, I will do a new thing; now it shall spring forth; shall ye not know it? I will even make a way in the wilderness, and rivers in the desert.

Isaiah 43:18-19

Another benefit of forgiveness is that OUR LORD JESUS CHRIST IS EXALTED! This is found in **Acts 5:31**.

Him hath God exalted with his right hand to be a Prince and a Saviour, for to give repentance to Israel, and forgiveness of sins.

Acts 5:31

Another benefit of forgiveness is that IT SETS YOU FREE! This is found in **John 8:36**.

If the Son therefore shall make you free, ye shall be free indeed.

John 8:36

And now that you are free, there are benefits of freedom too! That's why it's important to stay free and not allow anything to pull you back into unforgiveness.

Stand fast therefore in the liberty wherewith Christ hath made us free, and be not entangled again with the yoke of bondage.

Galatians 5:1

Now the Lord is that Spirit: and where the Spirit of the Lord is, there is liberty.

2 Corinthians 3:17

Freedom in your mind brings you peace.

And the peace of God, which passeth all understanding, shall keep your hearts and minds through Christ Jesus.

Philippians 4:7

Freedom in your body allows you to have good health.

Beloved, I wish above all things that thou mayest prosper *[live in the freedom of God]* and be in health, even as thy soul *[mind, will, and emotions]* prospereth.

3 John 2

Freedom in your spirit gives you life more abundantly, to the fullest.

…I am come that they might have life, and that they might have it more abundantly *[to the fullest]*.

John 10:10b

There are so many benefits to forgiveness and freedom! Continue to walk in the *Pain That Heals Unforgiveness*! Live the life God has promised and planned for you to live!

YOU DESERVE IT!!!!

YOU ARE HEALED!!!!

Even More Benefits of Forgiveness!

- Healthier relationships
- Improved mental health
- Less anxiety, stress, and hostility
- Lower blood pressure
- Fewer symptoms of depression
- A stronger immune system
- Improved heart health
- Improved self-esteem

SELF-REFLECTION

Journaling Page

Write down whatever comes to your heart and mind after reading this book.

Prayer of Thanksgiving

*Dear Heavenly Father,
I thank you for hearing and receiving all of my prayers
brought before you while reading this book.*

*I thank you for showing me all the areas of unforgiveness
that still remain in my heart.*

*Thank you, Lord, for forgiving me and for walking me
through the pain of unforgiveness.*

*Thank you, Lord, for walking with me,
even when I wasn't walking with you.*

*Thank you, Lord, for being here as I move forward and
walk through the* Pain That Heals Unforgiveness.

*Thank you, Lord, for loving me
and healing me today.*

*I know that I can do all things
through Christ who gives me strength.*

*Thank you, Lord for healing me!
In Jesus' Name! Amen!*

I can do all things through Christ which strengtheneth me.
Philippians 4:13

Whenever you pray for your healing, continue to work on yourself by getting and receiving the help you need **(James 2:17).**

You were not meant to walk through life alone. If you find yourself experiencing triggers and struggling with unforgiveness, please pray to God. If you are having a hard time praying, you can start by praying The Lord's Prayer **(Matthew 6:9-13).** God will lead you from there.

Then talk to someone, like a friend or relative that you can trust. You also can contact your Pastor (Pastors Team), a Counselor, a Therapist, or Group Therapist. These resources can be found through some employers, and also in your community, at schools and churches, and sometimes for a minimum fee or even free!

Be encouraged! God is working all things together for your good **(Romans 8:28).**

Know that when you decide to forgive, the process of forgiveness begins. No matter how long it takes, God will complete his work of forgiveness in you **(Philippians 1:6).**

Proverbs 34:17 – The righteous cry, and the Lord heareth, and delivereth them out of all their troubles.

Matthew 21:22 – And all things, whatsoever ye shall ask in prayer, believing, ye shall receive.

James 5:16 – Confess your faults one to another, and pray one for another, that ye may be healed. The effectual fervent prayer of a righteous man availeth much.

Proverbs 11:14 – Where no counsel is, the people fall: but in the multitude of counsellors there is safety.

Romans 8:28 – And we know that all things work together for good to them that love God, to them who are the called according to his purpose.

James 2:17 – Even so faith, if hath not works, is dead, being alone.

Philippians 1:6 – Being confident of this very thing, that he which hath begun a work in you will perform it until the day of Jesus Christ.

"...I am come that they might have life, and that they might have it more abundantly."
John 10:10b

The Beginning

Conclusion

The truth of the matter is we all will experience the pain of unforgiveness in this lifetime, and more often than we would like to. Every day we must make a conscious decision to forgive. In other words, we have to make up in our minds to forgive on purpose, knowing that this path of forgiveness is a journey. This journey is unpredictable, emotional, and different for each individual person, but it is also a journey that lasts a lifetime.

We must make a daily decision to forgive people, whether we know them personally or not. Yes! We must even choose to forgive the stranger who cuts us off while driving in traffic. We must consciously forgive the person who jumps in front of us in line at the grocery store. We must choose to forgive every single day. Otherwise we will find ourselves stuck in the pain of unforgiveness again.

To do this, we must believe in what our Lord and Savior Jesus Christ says in his Word (the Bible). We must know that no matter how we feel, what we see, what others say, or what's going on in our personal lives or the world today, God's Word is still true, and will always stand no matter what.

We must know, trust in, and **believe, accept,** and **receive** the truth that God loves us, and he is working all things together for our good **(Romans 8:28).**

Be encouraged! This is your new beginning! Continue to walk in the *Pain That Heals Unforgiveness.*

Everything you have endured, even what you are going through right now, is so you can help others on their journey to forgiveness as well, so they too can someday experience a new beginning.

Remember, God loves you. He is always with you, and he is working on your behalf.

And we know that all things work together for good to them that love God, to them who are the called according to his purpose.
Romans 8:28

The Spirit of the Lord GOD is upon me; because the LORD hath anointed me to preach good tidings unto the meek; he hath sent me to bind up the brokenhearted, to proclaim liberty to the captives, and the opening of the prison to them that are bound;

To proclaim the acceptable year of the LORD, and the day of vengeance of our God; to comfort all that mourn;

To appoint unto them that mourn in Zion, to give unto them beauty for ashes, the oil of joy for mourning, the garment of praise for the spirit of heaviness; that they might be called trees of righteousness, the planting of the LORD, that he might be glorified.
Isaiah 61:1-3

And Jesus came and spake unto them, saying, All power is given unto me in heaven and in earth.

Go ye therefore, and teach all nations, baptizing them in the name of the Father, and of the Son, and of the Holy Ghost:

Teaching them to observe all things whatsoever I have commanded you: and, lo, I am with you always, even unto the end of the world. Amen.

Matthew 28:18-20

Examples of Growth of Healing

- No longer afraid to get married
- No longer afraid to have meaningful relationships
- No longer struggling with an eating disorder
- No longer bound by addictions (alcohol, pornography, sex, gambling, shopping, etc.)
- Reunited in relationships that were meaningful
- No longer shutting down / refuse to talk / refuse to receive help
- No longer shutting people out and pushing people away
- The ability to believe in God again

Make a list of YOUR Points of Growth and Healing below.

References

Cole, Carliss. *Pain That Heals*. Witty Writings, 2011.

"Forgiveness: Letting go of grudges and bitterness". Healthy Lifestyle, Adult Health, Mayo Clinic. Last updated, November 13, 2020. *https://www.mayoclinic.org/healthy-lifestyle/adult-health/in-depth/forgiveness/art-20047692.* Accessed September 1, 2021.

Holy Bible, The, King James Version. Public Domain.

Oxford English Dictionary, https://languages.oup.com/dictionaries. Accessed September 1, 2021.

Quoted Scriptures

Chapter 1
Isaiah 53:5
John 10:10
Ephesians 3:20
3 John 2
2 Corinthians 5:7
Jeremiah 29:11
James 2:17
Matthew 6:9-13
Romans 8:28
Philippians 1:6
Psalm 34:17
Matthew 21:22
James 5:16
Proverbs 11:14
Romans 8:28
James 2:17
Philippians 1:6

Chapter 2
1 Peter 3:12
1 John 5:15
Jeremiah 29:12-13
John 3:17
James 2:17
Matthew 6:9-13

Chapter 2 (cont.)
Romans 8:28
Philippians 1:6
Psalm 34:17
Matthew 21:22
James 5:16
Proverbs 11:14
Romans 8:28
James 2:17
Philippians 1:6

Chapter 3
James 5:16
Proverbs 17:17
James 2:17
Matthew 6:9-13
Romans 8:28
Philippians 1:6
Proverbs 17:17
Psalm 34:17
Matthew 21:22
James 5:16
Proverbs 11:14
Romans 8:28
James 2:17
Philippians 1:6

Chapter 4
Proverbs 3:5-6
Ephesians 3:20
James 2:17
Matthew 6:9-13
Romans 8:28
Philippians 1:6
Matthew 18:21-22
Psalm 34:17
Matthew 21:22
James 5:16
Proverbs 11:14
Romans 8:28
James 2:17
Philippians 1:6

Chapter 5
Joel 2:25
Ephesians 3:20
Genesis 12:2
Romans 8:28
2 Corinthians 1:20
Matthew 22:37-39
James 2:17
Matthew 6:9-13
Philippians 1:6

Quoted Scriptures

Chapter 5 (cont.)
Psalm 34:17
Matthew 21:22
James 5:16
Proverbs 11:14
Romans 8:28
James 2:17
Philippians 1:6

Chapter 6
Proverbs 3:5
Proverbs 3:6
Matthew 22:37-38
John 14:15
Matthew 6:33
Matthew 18:21-22
Proverbs 14:14
Hebrews 13:5
Jeremiah 3:14
Deuteronomy 31:6
Matthew 28:20
Jeremiah 31:3
Job 1:20-22
2 Samuel 11:27
Job 42:10
1 Samuel 13:14

Chapter 6 (cont.)
Hebrews 4:15-16
Isaiah 53:3-5
John 1:1
John 1:14
Ezekiel 36:27
1 John 5:7
James 2:26
Romans 8:28
John 3:16
Isaiah 53:4-5
Hebrews 4:15
Isaiah 41:10
Numbers 23:19
2 Corinthians 1:20
Romans 5:8
James 2:17
Matthew 6:9-13
Romans 8:28
Philippians 1:6
Psalm 34:17
Matthew 21:22
James 5:16
Proverbs 11:14
Romans 8:28
James 2:17
Philippians 1:6

Chapter 7
John 8:3-11
Romans 3:23
Hebrews 12:6
John 3:17
1 Peter 5:7
Matthew 5:44
John 3:16
2 Corinthians 13:13
James 2:17
Matthew 6:9-13
Romans 8:28
Philippians 1:6
Philippians 3:13-14
2 Corinthians 5:17
Proverbs 34:17
Matthew 21:22
James 5:16
Proverbs 11:14
Romans 8:28
James 2:17
Philippians 1:6

Chapter 8
John 16:33
1 John 5:4

Quoted Scriptures

Chapter 8 (cont.)
Romans 12:21
1 John 4:4
1 John 5:5
Revelation 3:5
James 2:17
Matthew 6:9-13
Romans 8:28
Romans 12:21
Proverbs 34:17
Matthew 21:22
James 5:16
Proverbs 11:14
Romans 8:28
James 2:17
Philippians 1:6

Chapter 9
Romans 8:18
Matthew 6:15
Mark 11:25
1 John 1:9
Hebrews 8:12
Matthew 5:7
Psalm 130:4
2 Corinthians 5:17

Chapter 9 (cont.)
Philippians 4:7
3 John 2
John 10:10
Philippians 4:13
James2:17
Matthew 6:9-13
Romans 8:28
Philippians 1:6
Proverbs 34:17
Matthew 21:22
James 5:16
Proverbs 11:14
Romans 8:28
James 2:17
Philippians 1:6

About the Author

Carliss Cole is an ordained Evangelist and Minister, who believes in the complete healing power of God through sharing the promises of His word. She is a first-hand witness to miraculous healing; physically, mentally, emotionally, and spiritually. She is a published author and playwright whose writings address many common problems affecting families, people struggling in relationships and working in ministry, all while offering an uplifting message of hope through God's unfailing love. Carliss' passion to show God's unfailing love, inspired her to earn and receive her associate's, bachelor's, and master's degrees in communications. She is a published journalist and certified scriptwriter, who has written uplifting scripts for television, and inspiring columns in Sunday school manuals.

Carliss enjoys spending time with her family, watching movies, helping the homeless, tutoring children and adults, and providing college scholarship information opportunities to high school, college, and adult students. Carliss believes the trials and triumphs in her life are for the purpose of sharing and showing the love of Jesus Christ and to glorify God her heavenly Father. Carliss is a freelance writer and entrepreneur, who enjoys attending and serving under her Pastors David and Nicole Crank at Faith Church in St. Louis, Missouri. Her goal is to continue to show and share the love of Jesus Christ to the world, that many people can receive Jesus in their hearts, and live happy and fulfilling lives in him.

"I am come that they might have life, and that they might have it more abundantly."

John 10:10b